R₂cη

SOHO SQUARE V

EDITED BY STEVE KROMBERG & JAMES OGUDE

ILLUSTRATIONS JEFF FISHER

BLOOMSBURY

First published 1992
This compilation © 1992 by Bloomsbury Publishing Ltd
The copyright of the individual contributions remains
with the respective authors
The moral right of the authors has been asserted

Bloomsbury Publishing Ltd, 2 Soho Square, London W1V 5DE

A CIP catalogue record for this book
is available from the British Library

ISBN 0 7475 1332 5

10 9 8 7 6 5 4 3 2 1

Design and jacket by Jeff Fisher
Jacket photograph by Paul Hickman
Typeset by Hewer Text Composition Services, Edinburgh
Printed by Butler and Tanner Ltd, Frome and London

Contents

Introduction

Imagining and representing Africa is a complex affair. Too many editors have attempted to portray the 'essence of Africa' in ways that suit their own agendas, whether colonialist, nationalist, romantic or acquisitive.

Our brief from Bloomsbury was more modest: to compile an issue of *Soho Square* 'with an African flavour'. While we sought variation in theme, style and place of origin, our intention was not to produce an authoritative or thematically coherent anthology. We hoped that a loose, eclectic selection of contemporary unpublished work would allow African writers themselves to reveal diverse facets of their experiences.

Those contributors who are not from the continent have strong historical and emotional links with it. Sterling Plumpp and Frank Wilderson both write of their experiences on 'returning' to Africa from the United States. That most contributions are from South Africa is because we are based in Johannesburg. The continent is vast, communication difficult, and our task was further complicated by the shortage of time and limited financial resources. We nevertheless managed to include voices from the north, the west and the east.

The complex literary heritage that constitutes African creative writing is also reflected here. The writers draw on diverse styles and techniques, ranging from oral performance through the skilful merging of the oral and the literary, to pieces that lean heavily on the realist tradition. This is as it should be. The majority literary activity in Africa is oral and often remains a community activity in which the audience is an integral part of the performance. On the other hand, the letter was first formed on this continent; writing has both played an important role in Africa's cultural life and contributed significantly to the development of the colonial languages.

For most of these writers English is their second language; their contributions enrich English with local speech rhythms, idioms, imagery, and they often provide glimpses of African languages. Those who do not write in English have had their words translated.

As in previous issues of *Soho Square* we have included work by both 'established' and lesser-known voices. Creative talent in Africa is frequently frustrated by the shortage of publishing opportunities. We hope this edition of *Soho Square* will do something to redress the balance.

Some of the writing is provocative – and the ink is splashed in many directions. We have included it in the interests of reflecting at least some of the breadth, depth and complexity of the ideas found in this continent – and the many ways in which those ideas find themselves captured on paper. We kept editing to a minimum – in the hope of giving you, the reader, more to think about.

We hope that this taste of Africa's literary fare will whet the reader's appetite for more African writing and a deeper and more nuanced understanding of the continent. Such social and cultural dialogue can only benefit a continually shrinking world, in which it is tempting to reduce the 'other' to a one-dimensional character. Literature has the ability to take one beyond the thin representations that Western and African intellectuals and politicians have often constructed. What we would therefore stress is this collection's incompleteness; we like to think of it functioning to open a window rather than projecting a fixed, opaque image that says more about the flaws in the mirror than about the subjects being reflected.

As Nadine Gordimer argues, writing in Africa needs freedom if it is to thrive. This collection comes at a time when we are witnessing a resurgence of struggle for change in Africa. Some writers will be willing and able to play a role in that change. Others will choose to focus on more private and personal concerns, avoiding the overtly political in their writing. It is an essential part of the freedom – which has proved so tantalising and yet so elusive – that our writers be allowed to make this choice. We hope this spirit permeates the fifth edition of *Soho Square*.

We must thank the many people who gave us their time and encouragement. In particular we must mention Nadine Gordimer, Njabulo Ndebele, Richard Bartlett, José Luis Cabaço, Astrid von Kotze, the staff of the Congress of South African Writers and the New Nation (at whose conference we met a number of the writers represented here). The New Nation Writers' Conference was held in Johannesburg, 1–14 December 1991. The aim of the Conference was to draw international writers into a discussion on the writer's role in reconstruction, development and nation building.

MIA COUTO
Caramel Rose

Not much was known about her. She was known as the hunchback ever since she was a girl. We called her Caramel Rose. She was one of those upon whom another name is always bestowed. The one she had, the real one, just didn't do. If she was to live in the world it was more apt for her to be baptised again. And we didn't even want to accept something that sounded similar. She was Rose. Subtitle: Caramel. And we laughed.

Hunchback was a mixture of races, her body was the cross-breeding of many continents. As soon as she was ready for life her family left her. The place where she had slept since then wasn't much to look at. It was a hovel made of irregularly shaped boulders, with neither design nor proper height. Inside it not even the wood had evolved to the form of the plank: there was only the trunk, pure matter. Without bed or table the hunchback wasn't one to wait upon herself. Did she eat? No one had ever seen her with any sustenance. Even the eyes were meagre from that gauntness of wishing that one day they would be gazed at, with that rounded tiredness of having dreamt.

Her face, nevertheless, was pretty. Taken away from the body, it was even capable of kindling our desires. But if one looked at her from behind, and saw her in her fullness, such prettiness immediately ceased to exist. We saw her wandering on sidewalks, with her short, shuffling, steps. In the parks she would keep herself busy: she spoke to the statues. The worst was when she spoke to them of the sicknesses she suffered from. Everything else she did was clouded in silent secrecy, neither seen nor heard. But to exchange words with statues, not that, it was unacceptable. Because the spirit that went into the conversations was enough to frighten one. Did she want to cure the scar of the stones? With a motherly instinct she consoled each of the statues:

'Allow me, I'll clean you. I'm going to take away that dirt, it's their dirt.'

And she wiped the masonry bodies with a towel, filthy with dirt. Then she returned to the side-paths, now and then allowing herself to be guided by the circle of light shining from the lamp-posts.

During the day we forgot her existence. But at night the light of the moon confirmed for us the crookedness of her shape. The moon seemed to be stuck to the hunchback, like a coin in the hands of a miser. And, facing the statues, she sang in a hoarse and inhuman voice: she asked that they walk out of the stone. She overdreamt.

On Sundays she would retire, a nobody. The old woman disappeared, envious of those who filled the park, staining the restfulness of her territory.

Ultimately one didn't look for an answer to explain Caramel Rose. Only one motive could be reckoned with: at a certain time Rose had waited in suspense, flowers in her hand, at the entrance of the church. The bridegroom, the one that had been, was delayed. He was delayed for so long that he never arrived. He was the one who offered the suggestion: I don't want ceremony. You and I go, only the two of us. Witnesses? Only God, if he's free. And Rose implored:

'But what about my dream?'

All through her life she had dreamt of the wedding feast. A dream of splendour, of a retinue and guests. A moment that would be hers alone, she a queen, beautiful in the envy that spread all around her. With a long white dress, the outline of her back being corrected by a veil. Outside, a thousand hooters. And now, the fantasy was denied to her by the groom. If she could stop crying, to what avail would be loud presentations? She accepted. It would be done his way.

The hour came, the hour went. He neither came nor arrived. The curious onlookers drifted away, taking with them the laughter, the jeers. She waited, waited. No one had ever waited for so long. Only she had, Caramel Rose. She remained on the steps, as if they offered some consolation, reassurance, as if the stone sustained her universal disillusionment.

Stories people tell. Is there a grain of truth in them? It seems that there wasn't ever any bridegroom. She had got all that from her illusions. She had made herself bride. Rosie-the-courted, Rose-the-wed. But if nothing had happened, the outcome was hurtful enough. She had crippled herself for no good reason. To heal the ideas in her head they hospitalised her. But once they put her in hospital they didn't want to know her. Rose didn't get visitors, she never received the medicine of human fellowship. It suited her to be alone, away from people. She made herself sister to the stones, from leaning against them so often. Walls, floor, ceiling: only the stone gave her worth. Rosa laid herself, with the lightness of those who are in love, on the cold flooring. The stone, her twin.

On her discharge the hunchback went in search of her granite soul. It was then that she courted the solitary, reposeful statues. She gave them to drink (when they were thirsty), she protected them on rainy days, when it was cold. Her statue, the favoured one, was the one in the small park in front of our house. It was a monument to some colonial hero, the name of which wasn't even legible. Rose frittered away her time in contemplation of the bust. Love of no return: the man in the form of a statue always remained distant, never condescending to cast his gaze on the hunchback.

Sitting in our verandah, under the zinc roof of our wooden house, we would see her. My father, above all, would see her. He became speechless. Was it the madness of the hunchback that made us lose our reason? My uncle joked about and so saved the day:

'She's like the scorpion. She carries the poison on her back.'

We shared the laughter amongst ourselves. All of us, except for my father. He was completely left out, serious.

'No one sees her tiredness. Always carrying her back on her back.'

My father was much troubled by the sight of strange forms of weariness. He wasn't one to exhaust himself. Seated, he helped himself to many of life's calm moments. My uncle, a resourceful man, warned him:

'Brother Juca, find yourself some way of living.'

My father didn't even reply. It really looked as though he'd become, himself, leaned back, an accomplice of the old chair. Our uncle was right: he needed a salaried job. His only diligence was hiring out his own shoes. On Sunday his friends from the club stopped by on the way to the soccer match.

'Juca, we came 'cause of the shoes.'

He nodded, with extreme slowness.

'You know the deal: you take them and then, when you come back, you tell me how the game went.'

He bowed down to remove the shoes under the chair. He lowered himself with such effort it looked as though he was trying to catch the very floor. He lifted the pair of shoes and feigned a goodbye as he looked at them:

'It's really hard on me.'

18

He only stayed at home because of the doctor. Too much strain on the heart, on the flow of the blood, had been forbidden to him.

'Rubbish heart.'

He beat at his breast to punish the organ. He then turned to the shoes, and chatted to them:

'Watch well, my little shoes: at the right time you come back home.'

And he received the money, in advance. He counted the money, slowly, with drawn-out gestures. It was as if he were reading a fat book, one of those that favour the fingers more than the eyes.

My mother: she was the one that stepped out into the world. She was out early in the morning, on her way. The morning was still young when she got to the market. The world was barely visible during the early morning rehearsal of the sun. Mother cleaned her stand before the other sellers did. Behind the heaps of cabbages was her face, a fat face of many sad silences. There she sat, both her and her body. In life's struggle mama had somehow eluded us. She arrived and she left in the dark. At night we heard her, scolding father's laziness.

'Juca, do you think about life?'

'I think much about life.'

'Sitting down?'

My father's replies were sparse. She, and only she, complained:

'I am alone, I work inside, I work outside.'

Bit by bit, the voices in the corridor dies down. My mother still uttered a few sighs, swoons of hope. But we never blamed our father. He was a good man. So good that he could never defend himself.

And life in our small district continued very much the same. Until one day we received the news: Caramel Rose had been arrested. Her only offence: the veneration of a colonialist. The head of the militia ascribed the sentence to: longing for the past. The madness of the hunchback was merely the cover for other, political, reasons. So said the commander. If it wasn't that, what other motive would she have in opposing, with violence, with her whole body, the demolishing of the statue? Yes, because that monument was a foot from the past leaving its tracks in the present time. For respect for the nation to be preserved it was necessary to press for the decapitation of the statue.

So they took old Rose away, so they could cure these alleged thoughts of hers. It was only then, in her absence, we saw how much she filled our landscape.

For a long time we heard no news. Until one afternoon my uncle broke the silence. He had come from the graveyard, from the burial of Jawane, the male nurse. He climbed the small steps of the verandah, interrupting my father's rest. Scratching his legs, my old man blinked his eyes, gauging the amount of light:

'And so, did you bring the shoes?'

My uncle didn't answer at first. He was making use of the shade, relieving himself of the sweat. He blew air into his very lips, tired. In his face I could see the relief of someone who has returned from a funeral.

'Here they are, brand new. Gee man, Juca, these black shoes were really useful!'

He searched his pockets, but the money, always quick to get in, took a long time to come out. My father saved him from further searches:

'To you I didn't hire them. We're family, we wear them together.'

My uncle sat down. He poured a bottle of beer into a big glass. Then, with great skill, he took a wooden spoon and with it removed the foam, placing it in another glass. My father took this glass, the one only with foam. Liquids being forbidden to him, the old man devoted himself to the foamy.

'It's so light, this foaminess. The heart doesn't even feel it going through.'

He consoled himself, his eyes steady, as if he wished to lengthen the thought. They were no more than a fake, those reflections.

'Were there lots of people at the burial?'

While untying the shoes, my uncle described the throng of people, the crowds trampling over the flower beds, all of them saying farewell to the nurse; poor man, he had himself died.

'But did he really kill himself?'

'Yeah, the guy hanged himself. When they found him he was hard already, as if he was starched hanging from the rope.'

'But he killed himself for what reason?'

'Who knows. They say it was because of women.'

The two of them were quiet, sipping from their glasses. What hurt them the most was not the fact of the death but the motive for it.

'To die like that? It's better to pass away.'

My old man received the shoes and surveyed them distrustfully:
'This sand comes from there?'
'Where's it, that there?'
'I'm asking if it comes from the graveyard.'
'Maybe it comes.'
'Then go clean it. I don't want the dust of the dead here.'

My uncle walked down the steps and sat on the last one, brushing the soles of the shoes. In the meantime he went on telling the story. The ceremony was still going on, the priest said the prayers, blessing the souls with them. All of a sudden, what happens? There arrives Caramel Rose, all dressed up in mourning black.

'Has Rose already left prison?' asked my father (in a voice without tone).

Yes, she had. During an inspection of the prison she had been granted amnesty. She was mad, she wasn't guilty of any serious crime. My father pressed for more, astonished:

'But her, in the cemetery?'

My uncle continued with the account. Rose, from her back down, all in black. Not even a raven, Juca. She went in, spying the graves as if she were a grave-digger. It looked as if she was choosing her own hole. You know, Juca, in the cemetery no one spends much time checking out the excavations. We do it quickly. But this hunchback, she . . .

'Tell me the rest,' cut in my father.

The story went on: standing there, Rose started singing in front of everybody. The mourners just stared at her, bewildered. The priest was still praying, but no one paid any attention to him any more. It was then that the hunchback started undressing.

'You lie, brother.'

'True's God, Juca, two thousand knives will fall on me if I lie.' She undressed. She started removing her clothes, more slowly than the heat of the day. No one laughed, no one coughed, nobody nothing. When she was naked, without any clothes, she moved close to Jawane's grave. She lifted her arms and threw the clothes over the hole. The sight made the mourners take fright, and they took a few steps back. Rose then prayed:

'Take these clothes, Jawane, you'll need them. Because you're going to be stone like all the others.'

Looking at the spectators, she raised her voice, a voice higher than that of any living creature:

'And now: am I allowed to like?'

The mourners retreated, and only the voice of dust spoke to them.

'Not so? I can like this dead one! He's not in time any more. Or is this one also forbidden to me?'

My father rose from his chair; he was almost offended.

'Did Rose speak like that?'

'It's genuine.'

And the uncle, ready already, copied the hunchback, her squint body: and this one, can I love him? But my old man would not listen.

'Stop, I won't hear any more.'

He spoke so brusquely that his glass fell out of his hands into the air. He wanted to pour out the foam but because of an unfortunate slip the whole thing fell. And as if he were apologising, my uncle picked up the small shards of glass, tumbled upside down throughout the yard.

That night I was unable to sleep. I got out of the house, trying to give the insomnia a rest in the park. I looked at the statue; it had been removed from the pedestal. The colonial had his beard on the ground, and it looked as if he had himself climbed down, so tired of it all. They had pulled down the monument but had forgotten to remove it; the work needed some finishing off. I almost felt sorry for the bearded man, made dirty by the pigeons, covered with dust. Then I switched on, I came to my senses: I'm like Rose, putting feelings into boulders? It was then that I saw Caramel herself, as if my conjuring had beckoned her. I almost froze, unable to move. I wanted to run away, but my legs wouldn't take me. I shuddered: I was becoming a statue, I was turning into the object of the hunchback's affections? Horror, I would never speak again. But, no. Rose didn't stop in the park. She crossed the seat and moved towards the little steps of our house. She lowered herself towards the steps and cleaned the moonlight that shone on them. All her life seemed to dwell in a single sigh. She then huddled herself like a turtle, preparing herself, who knows what for, sleepiness. Or perhaps her only resolve was to feel sadness. For I heard her crying, the murmur of dark waters. The hunchback wept; it looked like her turn to become a statue. A boundless countenance.

It was then my father, with an afflicting silence, opened the door of the verandah. Slowly, he approached the hunchback. For a while he leaned over the woman. Then moving his hand, in the gesture of something long dreamt of, he stroked her hair. In the beginning Rose didn't even move. But, later, she began crawling out of herself, half her face in the light. They gazed at each other, gaining a particular beauty. He then whispered:

'Don't cry, Rose.'

I almost didn't hear, my heart leapt up to my ears. I moved closer, always behind the darkness. My father still spoke to her, a kind of voice I had never heard before.

'It's me, Rose. You don't remember?'

I was right in the middle of the bougainvillaea, its thorns tore at me. I didn't even feel them. The dismay jabbed harder than the branches. The hands of my father were drowning in the hunchback's hair, they looked like people, those hands, like people drowning.

'It's me, Juca. Your bridegroom, don't you remember?'

Bit by bit Caramel Rose came to her senses. Never had she felt so intensely about life, no statue had ever deserved such a gaze from her eyes. His voice ever more sweet, my father called out:

'Let's go, Rose.'

Effortless, I walked away from the bougainvillaea. They could see me, it wouldn't embarrass me. When the hunchback rose it was as if the light of the moon had been roused.

'Let's go, Rose. Pick up your things, let's go away.'

And the two of them went, walking into the night.

translated by Luís Rafael

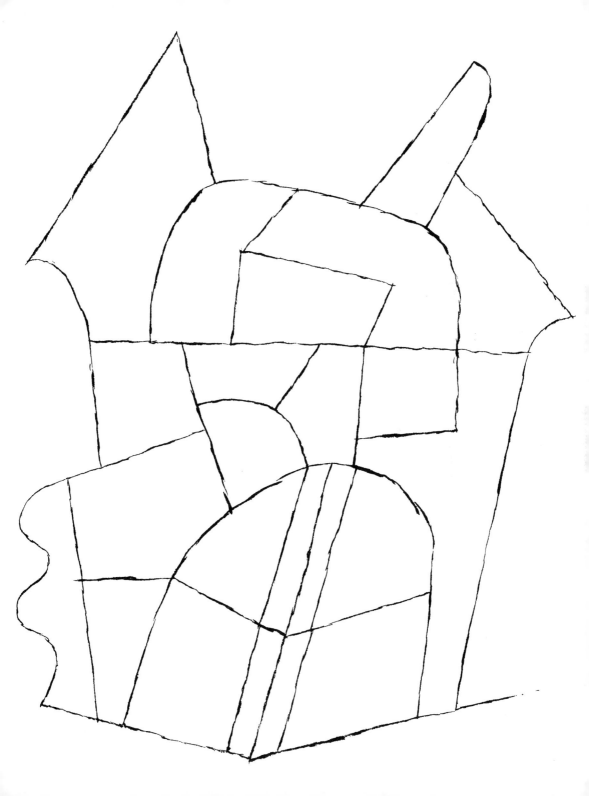

JONATHAN KARIARA
And You, Africa

I have felt you slip
From a tentative foot
Not emboldened by the years.
I gasped,

In fear of drowning,
And I still must feel
For firm ground
Grope for some anchored sport

To fix my foot.
These muffled noises around me
Do not signify deafness.
The eye, though weary,

Still sees.
There is a fuming in the head,
A throbbing in the temples
Waves of darkness invade,

Body flushes and releases
Warm, clammy sweat.
There is a smell of ether here.
Cotton wool plugging the orifices.

A face, startled into death,
Fixed in a green stillness,
Hints of moist, mossy places.
This is not harmony.

There is even less meaning here
Than we dare admit.
The coffin is adorned
And so is the bride.

Only,
The music is tired,
A suppressed yawn threatens
To burst into a scream.

It's not even you
That I'm talking to.
My address
Is to the mad man in town

Whose haunches have swelled with useless possessions
Whose wanderings in a city
Set for flight
Are a perfect parable of you.

AMA ATA AIDOO
Heavy Moments

Akuba opened the door to the toilet near the cockpit. She had almost waited too long. Because she was now having to do a little *tinawale* jig. Left foot down, right foot up. So that she would not wet herself. There was no time at all for her to stop and wonder at the phenomenon. How could this happen to her of all people? Her Mampa had always warned her against what she described as Akuba's habit of senselessly and uselessly hoarding her urine. 'One of these days, you are going to burst your bladder.'

Akuba nearly choked on that. Oh Mampa, she thought fondly. She was also remembering that it was the same Mampa she had once overheard mutter to herself in the face of some crisis that we meet our in-laws only when we are in our farming rags. Or something to that effect. And in any case, is this the time to remember all these things? But the mind is a funny thing. So she went on remembering as she struggled out of the trousers of her uniform. She had worn a brand new pair. Which in retrospect could not have been the wisest thing to do. The zipper was proving difficult . . . please God, don't let it break. Please God, don't . . . then the trousers were unzipped, she was sitting on the toilet, and peeing what appeared to be all the clear fluids from her body. This was obviously a morning of surprises.

Now where had she heard the one about the old man who in an argument as to whether women should wear trousers, had calmly declared, puffing on his pipe, that it should not really be a problem for anybody but women themselves? 'If they want to imitate men. Fine. They'll find out whether they should wear trousers when they want to urinate!'

Enjoying the release of the tension at the bottom of her belly, she flushed the toilet, washed her hands, shut the door of the toilet and returned to the cockpit. She sat down, smiled at her co-pilot and took the controls.

The captain nearly made some comment about women. But he bit his tongue. Biting his tongue had almost become a habit in the past couple of years that he had had those two among his recruits at the Air Force Academy. Suddenly, everything had changed completely.

Whereas, before, you could say anything you liked about women and be sure of sympathetic ears and a good laugh, these days you had to watch everything: your step, your mouth and over your shoulder.

Earlier, they had thought it wouldn't matter. But it had come to matter. Terribly. At first, an alarm sounded through the academy when first the rumours, then later the hard facts, had come out. Two of the very best candidates that year were women.

'Women?'

'Women?'

'But . . . but . . . but . . .'

'What do they want here?'

'What do they want here?'

'What   do   they   want   here?'

Everybody had asked the same questions. From retired Group Captains who had only heard of it in the mess which was still their home from home, to those recruits who were as new to the academy as the young women themselves. It had never occurred to the questioners that Akuba Baidoo and Sarah Larbi wanted from the Academy what they too had gone there for. That if being a flying soldier was something to be enjoyed and lived by, then other people – including women – could want it too.

They had even tried to ignore the two young women recruits and carry on as if they were not around at all. Or at best as if the two were men too. So during the first term even those who would ordinarily not have been given to telling lewd jokes went around looking for someone to tell. Especially when 'Cadet Baidoo' and 'Cadet Larbi' were around. And no one had liked it that 'the girls' did not laugh.

At the end of the semester, Akuba and Yaa Sarah had complained to the Director of the Academy. He himself had been one of the worst offenders. So although he had been careful not to tease 'the girls' to their faces, he had listened them out, and tried to pretend that he had not the slightest idea of what they were talking about. It didn't work. So he had promised he would do something about it. He subsequently called his lieutenants, spoke to them, and asked them to speak to their men. There followed a period when, except demanded by the most formal of circumstances, virtually no one spoke to them at the academy. When they compared notes during that time and later, each of them made an admission. That if she had been alone, she would have given up and left. But luckily they were two. So sticking it out had been a little easier.

And now here is Akuba handling the manual controls of an air force plane, as though she had been born flying. Good God, a woman. Wonders surely would never cease.

Actually, Akuba had been born flying. Except that, given her environment, no one had known that except herself. Her maternal grandparents' village lay in the path of the planes that flew over coastal West Africa: from southern and central Africa on their way to North Africa and beyond to Europe, as well as those that flew from those northern places to the south. One of the most enduring memories from her childhood was of her and a group of children from the neighbourhood watching those planes. In that, she was certain that the earliest sound she had caught as a foetus in her mother's womb was the drone of a plane passing over the distant skies . . . Now she knew that these planes flew at over thirty thousand feet. But clearly that had not stopped her and her friends from rushing out if it was during the day, and screaming their usual chorus:

'Aeroplane el!
ekor aa to paano
   brem oo!'

'Dear plane, dear plane,
(on your return journey)
buy some bread and
bring to me, oo!'

It was quite possible that for some of the other children it had just been another game. Maybe for others it had been an expression of a desire to travel? Because one didn't have to send a plane that high up and so far away for bread? Since Aunti Araba baked the best bread in the world right there in the village? Besides, there were several more bakers in Dominase. And one had not even gone as far as Mankessim and Oguaa yet. Where for sure there were so many bakers you sometimes wondered who bought whose bread? But she also remembered that grown-ups always said that whatever came from overseas was very special. So maybe that included b-r-e-a-d?

However, as far as she was concerned, aeroplanes had always meant something different.

She had wanted to fly them.

The desire had been in her for so long, she could not tell how young she was when she became aware of it. All she knew was that one night – it must have been deep deep in the night – she had woken up suddenly to what was unmistakably the sound of a passing plane. And then she knew she wished she was up there flying it. When the sound of the plane died, she started to cry. When her big mother Mam'Panyin asked her what the matter was, she couldn't speak. She just sat there wailing. In exasperation, Mampa had called her a witch of a child, wailing in the middle of the night. Did she know it was taboo? A bad omen? Because all the bad spirits would come and join in, and then someone in the house or neighbourhood was bound to die for sure? When she still couldn't stop crying, Mampa had given her a surprising knock on the head. So Akuba had bitten her tongue and wet herself. Mampa had felt so bad, she had taken Akuba in her arms and rocked her, and started to cry herself. Because you see, even as a young child, Akuba never wet herself. It was a terrible night. Finally, both of them slept again only in the early hours of the morning. But she had never forgotten that night, and now here she was actually flying a plane and so excited she nearly peed herself.

She wondered whether they marked a pilot down for letting go of the controls in order to attend to urgent bodily functions? She sincerely hoped they didn't. After all, one was allowed time for such vagaries of the human body during all other serious examinations she knew and had heard of. So why not this one? Maybe they'd hold it against her for being a woman? She'd worry about all of that later. This was a complete manual affair. Nothing was on auto. So she had better concentrate.

She was lucky. At mid-morning in September, the sky was brilliantly blue. And although they were about fifteen thousand feet up, they could see into everywhere and for ever. Ahead, the sea that was the Gulf of Guinea reflected the brilliance of the sky. To the right and left, the forest was giving way to low savannah. She knew she would have to get ready to land the plane very soon. She was almost sorry. Not almost. She wished the plane was one of those futuristic self-fuelling machines that could go for ever on ordinary air. Or at least, one of those then being planned for American presidents which its designers claimed would be able to refuel in midair, and then fly non-stop for eight days or something monstrous like that.

Supposing she failed? She panicked so much she nearly made a mistake. She bit her lips. Her hands were shaking, and she soon began to sweat. She told herself not to be silly. If she failed, she would take the exam again. Then she reminded herself that given their environment, getting a place in the academy at all was hard enough. She was not sure they let people stay there forever, taking their own good time to graduate. And had she forgotten she was a woman? One of the first two ever in the history of the academy? How would her failure be regarded as personal and nothing to do with her gender? All in all, she had better pass this test.

Until she came to understand it all later, she had always assumed that Mam'Panyin was her grandmother. But it had turned out she was not. She was her mother's oldest sister: her grandmother's first child. And in fact, that was why everyone called her Big Mother. There had been about seven or eight more children between Mam'Panyin and her mother. Her mother had been the last but one of her grandmother's children. The last, a boy, had been so big, her poor grandmother had died during his birth. Or soon after.

. . . As for her mother, who was then only two years old, they had packed her off to the coastal town of Sekunde: to a distant educated relative who had promised to look after her like her own. But in the end the educated relative had just used the little orphan, as soon as she could run and fetch, as a slave for her household. So the child that was to be Akuba's mother was never put in school for even a day. But the relative's children had gone on to become doctors, laywers and such . . .

Then one day the little orphan had bloomed into a young beautiful woman, and the next, a young railway worker in the neighbourhood had made her pregnant. When the educated relative discovered the pregnancy, she had packed Akuba's mother back to the village. When Akuba's natural father journeyed to the village to get things sorted out properly, her mother's people had refused to give him even a place to sit down. Hearing him out was out of the question. How could they marry their princess to someone who lived in a city where human beings could be so cruel? No way . . . They say Akuba's natural father later drank himself to death.

After Akuba was born, her mother, who had been hurt and hurt and hurt by all these goings on, decided to take her child back with her into town. And things had gone well with mother and child until Akuba's mother married. And then the man said he didn't want Akuba around. Whereupon she was sent back to the village, where she went to school until she was about twelve years old.

Then, marriage or no marriage, Akuba's mother decided that Akuba should go back to live with her and take the Common Entrance Examinations. So that was how she got into secondary school. But her stepfather hadn't really changed. Except to indicate that if he had to have her around, then he would sleep with her. And if she would not let him, which Akuba would not, then he would beat her to death. That was the last time Akuba saw her mother's house in Sekunde. She never set foot there again. From boarding school, Akuba went straight to Mam'Panyin at the village, deciding somewhere along the way that if she had got parents in this world, it must be Mam'Panyin for a father and Mam'Panyin for a mother. But as a kid she had never been able to say 'Mam'Panyin'. She had arbitrarily abbreviated it to 'Mampa'. And so that's how the whole village came to call Mam'Panyin 'Mampa'.

It was all very well for Mampa to complain about Akuba behaving as though she belonged in the air. But the fact was that Akuba did feel airborne. Always. Or something like that anyway. She had never felt rooted. She had never felt like she belonged on the ground. There had been this business of getting passed around all through her childhood, between the village and the town. And of course when she was in the village, everyone accused her of having 'funny town ways'. And when she was in town, everyone had laughed at her for being 'bush', 'a villager'! Not having 'a proper mother' or a 'proper father' like everyone else, was only part of the story.

Poor Akuba. She could not have known, could she, that in any group of people, one clear quarter or more were in some similar situation?

No, the skies had to be better.

Of course, there was a bit of a crisis when Akuba went to tell Mampa that she had been accepted at the Air Force Academy. Mampa thought it was all too much.

'I say,' Mampa said, 'if I told people that you are going to learn to drive a lorry, a taxi or a bus, they would think it is strange, but brave achievement enough for a woman. But how do you expect me to go

35

and tell everybody that you are actually going to drive an aeroplane through the skies and be believed? And if they won't believe me, what's the use in trying to tell them? Eh, my lady?'

They had planned everything. That her test flight should be on that day. It was risky. You took such chances only with the best of the cadets, since you had to be able to guarantee success on about 90% probability. But then Baidoo was one such cadet. They were very sure of her. And Cadet Larbi and such among the male cadets who could remotely be described as Baidoo's friends had said how much Akuba loved her aunt, and was always talking about her. So the administration had decided that since this was going to be a rare enough occasion, testing a female cadet pilot (!), they might as well go all the way and do something extra special. They would let this lady know about Akuba's test flight: the date, the time, everything. Yes, they would take the responsibility to alert her, and leave it to her to decide whether to come to the air force base or not.

The voice from the control tower came over the radio clearly, helping, guiding. She began gently to nose down . . .

Then she was actually taxiing on the airstrip. She brought the plane to a stop. She realised that there was quite a crowd waiting for her. In no time at all, the captain and everyone who had been on board was already on the tarmac, looking up at her as she came down. And they started clapping, and then the small crowd at the edge of the airstrip was also clapping. All her colleagues were there. Each one of them. Those who had already had their tests, and the rest who had been scheduled to come after her. They were all there. Waiting. Then someone broke into that mad English song. 'For she's a jolly good fellow . . .' Everyone took the song up. And she wanted to tell them, 'Silly, can't you see I am not a "fellow" at all? Jolly or not?'

How had all these men managed to change so much in such a short time? After all they had put her and Yaa through? How could they show their joy for her so clearly? And by the way, where was Cadet (Yaa) Sarah Larbi . . . where was Yaa Sarah? Akuba wanted to burst into tears, with both joy and . . . yes, disappointment. God, where was Yaa Sarah? Someone was opening a bottle of champage. Then she could see Sarah coming out of the crowd. Ow-w-w, what a relief! And with her an older woman. And ow . . . it's Mampa, Mampa, Mampa . . .

WILMA STOCKENSTRÖM
Africa Love

Like Inhaca facing the coast, I'm turned
to you, with my soft mouth, my breasts.
Like her I nestle in a bay of kindness,
I grow, coral-like but without fail
closer to you, my mainland. What
does the mercantile marine back
on the battering seas mean to me?
Cunningly my dripping mangroves advance
in tepid waters step by little step.
How long before I merge with your wide
cashew-nut forests, before we fit into each other,
your reed-overgrown arm around me,
your brown body my body.

translated by Johann de Lange

STERLING PLUMPP
Weaver
(for Zim Ncqwana)

Your
spiralled agony,
your remembered speech
to the Gods of Every Day.
March
in your tone.
How
did you
get from here
to Harlem and
back on a
Trane.
Where I hold
reservations on your Express Distanced Voyager.
And now travel
over
the shadows I saw
darting
through blackness
in Alexandra.
Darting
through nights and
nights.
I know.
The signatures of pain
scribbled on wind.
I have
known in runawayed flights

from chains and
changed names.
The
Sometimes I Feel Like A Motherless Child
fisted cries.
I know.
You
voyage from lynch ropes
to the sprawling metaphors of
Soweto.
Nights and
nights in silence.
The
boy shot in the head on my Chicago block.
You
play his cry in longings
where the eclipse of your rhythms.

Pummel
horrors outside the door of
my mind

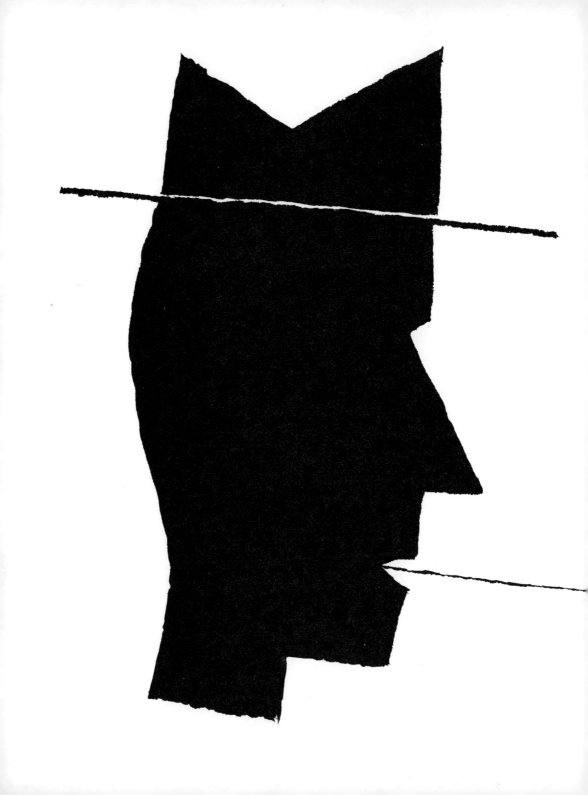

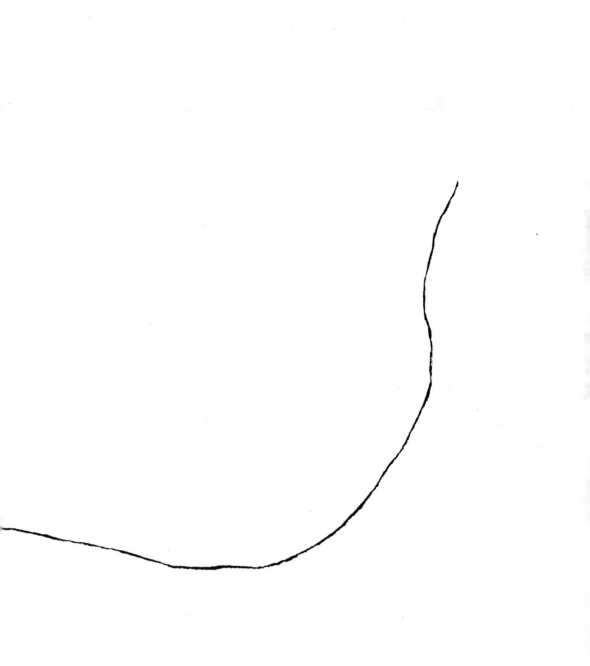

SHIMMER CHINODYA
Among the Dead

When Mr Melbury breathed his chest whistled as if he was sucking pins through his nostrils. When he spoke his voice squeaked like a guitar making a chord, then it broke into the finest English accent I had heard.

Mr Melbury was a short man, hardy and a little stout, with a flag of silver hair on his balding head. He had a small beaked nose and thin pale lips which popped into a glistening pink smile. His arms were short like clubs, petering amazingly into fine long fingers. His darting blue eyes concluded his resemblance to a bird.

If you stood face to face with him, not too far away, it was almost possible to think he might have been handsome as a young man. It was almost possible to forget he was a hunchback, until he turned round and the deformity stuck out at you. If you stood near him and heard the air hissing into him, stabbing into his lungs, and you saw the protrusion at his back heaving with each breath he took, you might even wonder how he had lived seventy years like that. It was if a coat-hanger had been wrenched through him and he was pitched forward along an invisible rail by some electrical force.

I have always had this pity for hunchbacks. Much as I try to stifle it, it rears its head every time, urging me to open doors or stand back or perform some other clumsily vague gesture of kindness, as if I need to apologise for my physical well-being.

One morning I saw Mr Melbury walking ahead of me in the corridor, carrying some books to our geography class. Sidling up beside him, I asked to carry his books for him. He turned sharply at me, his blue eyes trembling, something ticking like a time bomb inside him. He walked a dozen more steps without saying a word then cracked crisply, 'No thank you. I always carry my own books. I can manage.'

I fell back and dodged behind his heels, feeling furious with myself. Realising I should never have dared to feel sorry for him, I vowed to steer clear of him.

But even before I asked to carry his books, Mr Melbury had already developed a devilish interest in me. I was a new student at the school all right but I was convinced he had set me up as some kind of target. I knew from the way he lingered over my back while the class worked at an assignment, the way he always got me to answer questions in class, watching me with those deadly knowledgeable airs while I floundered in doubt, that he enjoyed cornering me.

He knew the geography teacher at my old school had been the author of a prescribed textbook which most classes in the country were using. I slowly discovered that Mr Melbury had a personal feud with that author, with whom he disagreed on certain academic matters referring to that book. I began to suspect that he saw me as a disciple of that author in whose place I could be rightly persecuted.

'Come on,' he would taunt, 'you were taught by a famous textbook writer. What did that famous writer say about the geomorphological causes of the East African Rift Valley?' Or: 'What is your author's considered opinion about the existence of Gondwanaland?'

Now I knew Gondwanaland was something to do with the theory of continental drift, based on the belief that Africa, South America and Australia might have once existed as one continent. I knew the theory well but could not tie it up with the name, much to Mr Melbury's amusement.

'Taught by the famous geographer and you can't explain Gondwanaland! Come on class, somebody explain to him what the word means . . .'

Don't get me wrong. Mr Melbury was an accomplished scholar and a brilliant teacher, though he had not published any books. I respected him as a teacher. He gave numerous assignments which he promptly marked and returned. Hating research work as I did, preferring to spend more time on literature and writing, I chose one week to write for him an account of wine production in Southern Africa. Fatally entitling my work 'Wine Growing in Southern Africa', I proceeded to assemble hastily concocted notes into solid looking prose, broken optimistically by maps and diagrams.

Three days later, I received back the assignment with a generous paragraph of Mr Melbury's immaculate red cursive:

A very gallant attempt to conquer the unknown. Unfortunately chivalric excursions like this often end in catastrophe. This essay is so beautifully written, so marvellously full of cadence, but totally misleading. The maps and diagrams are pretty but woefully outdated. Perhaps what disturbed me most when I read your essay was my ignorance of the fact that farmers in Southern Africa could actually *grow* wine . . .

After reading the comment I looked up and saw Mr Melbury gloating at me from across the room with that look that seemed to say, 'There, I got you now!'

I had been at the mission school for only three weeks, preparing for my university entrance examination two months away. The war was intensifying. Under a barrage of guerrilla attacks the beast of Rhodesia was sagging to its knees. Large tracts of the country were falling into the war zone.

I had just been expelled from a government high school, together with a hundred other sixth-formers, for staging peaceful demonstrations against government moves to conscript black school-leavers into the Rhodesian army. We had marched forty miles at night to stage the demonstration, got harassed by the police and unceremoniously expelled from school. After the expulsions some of my classmates had crossed the border to join the guerrillas. Others had vanished into crowded suburbs or half-known villages. A handful, like me, had been lucky enough to secure places at more sympathetic mission schools.

I was still bristling with the anger of Rhodesia and had developed a venomous desire to be left alone. Naturally, I quickly took offence.

Even then I knew my anger towards Mr Melbury was to an extent irrational. After all, the mission school he worked for had accepted me. Although he himself was not in the order, he had lived and worked at the mission for over forty years. In that sense, he was a missionary and mission teachers were in those days regarded as liberals. But Rhodesia had taught me to see things in terms of black and white. Like wounded prey I was wary, suspicious, ready to take offence at the slightest provocation.

I knew I had made a mess of the essay but the sarcastic edge in Mr Melbury's comments, the way he turned what should have been straightforward criticism into an exhibition of his formidable literary armoury, cut me deeply. I knew I could write better essays and I hated to think he took me for a fool. I withdrew into silence. Just to prove I was no fool I wrote better essays to which he conceded 'A's. I noticed his taunts relent a little. One Sunday after the morning service he came up behind and said unexpectedly:

'Oh, you have such a deep voice which can go to great depths. Would you like to join the mission choir?'

I turned to look at him, surprised. His blue eyes were still. I had not noticed before that his eyelashes were turning grey. His pale lips hung open, the bristling tongue poised – charged, I supposed – with a fresh insult. I could hear his chest sputter.

'The choir . . .' I stammered, wrestling with myself. 'I really don't know. I would need to think about it, I suppose.'

'Ho. I see you need to think about it. We'd be happy to have you in the choir.'

As a young boy I had once sung in a church choir but I was not sure I wanted to join the mission choir. I was new at the mission school and wanted to maintain my anonymity. I took pride in not allowing myself to be swallowed by the rituals of mission-school life.

Later that week, on All Souls' Day, the school went down to the cemetery to pray for the dead. It was a bright blue morning – piety seemed to hang in the air. Like butterflies, boys and girls swarmed over the graves. Some people sat on the rocks, some in the passageways and others leaned on tombstones. I was loitering at the edge of the cemetery, among the rocks, when Mr Melbury came up from behind me. I couldn't evade him. He had spotted me already.

'I don't think you had rituals such as these at your previous school,' he said.

'No,' I told him.

'Then you must find life here very strange.'

'Sometimes.'

His chest was sputtering again. It seemed he was humming softly to himself, under his breath. His lips hung open. I wasn't sure if he was grinning or grimacing.

'There's plenty of sitting space among the graves,' he said. I shrugged.

'You can even sit on the tombstones if you like.'

'I'm all right here,' I said.

'Perhaps you resent sitting among the dead?'

'Oh, no – !'

'You are superstitious?'

'Not really.'

'Why should you be afraid of the dead, then?'

'I'm not afraid of the dead. It's just that . . . I respect them.'

I have always had this reverent dislike for graveyards, based on a healthy fear of coffins and corpses.

Even then I had weaned myself of childish taboos that had been hammered on us – the belief that your finger would fall off if you pointed at a grave, for instance, or that your feet would have scabs and fall off if you walked over it – those taboos surely permeating every culture in one form or another – generated to inspire not so much fear as respect. I could not explain to Mr Melbury then that my fear was based on a strong personal belief that the human soul was too strong to be annihilated by death. It wasn't a belief in religion or in the afterlife or anything like that – it was just my belief, in which hauntings and visitations were not altogether impossible.

'If you are not superstitious would you like to come with me on a midnight tour of this graveyard tonight?'

'Why?' I managed a little laugh.

'Just to prove superstition is completely unfounded. That graveyards are just like any other place – '

'Well – ' I shrugged again.

The ritual was beginning and he seated himself on a flat-topped boulder next to me. The crowd quietened down among the tombstones. The choir, conducted by a hyperactive, red-haired nun, swept into melody.

Early one Saturday morning I had seen the same nun going up to the geography room with Mr Melbury. He had worn a faded brown suit and from the bottom of the steps I had seen the nun's vest, like wire gauze, through her dress. They had talked in tones too low for my inquisitive ears. Always the nun wore that gauze-like vest and I wondered if she had anything else underneath. I knew Mr Melbury ate with the nuns sometimes, at the rectory. I had been to the dining room once and glimpsed the tables draped with the white cloth, laid out with spotless cutlery and jars of water. It was a cold scene somehow – everything spick and span. The only thing that had excited me was the bowl of crimson apples and the loaf of brown bread, though the bread had vaguely reminded me of the Last Supper. I had come away wondering what ever made people want to join the order.

The choir finished their song, wrenching me back to the present. This was followed by litanies. Then the priest lit the incense and walked up and down the cemetery, letting the holy grey smoke diffuse into the wide expanse.

A quiet murmur rippled through the graveyard. I liked the smell of incense and the sense of the imaginative and the mysterious it invoked. I thought even the church, too, was riddled by little acts of superstition such as these and, wondering how Mr Melbury would react to this allegation, chose quietly to draw in deep breaths of incense until the ritual ended.

He came for me at a quarter to twelve that night.

I was in my study cubicle working on my assignment when I heard him sputter and crackle behind me. I was surprised he came. I thought he had proposed the tour as a joke, but there he was, gloating down at me with twinkling eyes, his hands thrust challengingly into the pockets of his coat. I closed my books and followed him out of the study block, away from the perimeter of light, into the night. I didn't have to slow down; he thrust himself forward resolutely, as we went through the grove, past the chapel looming dark and medieval and the dormitories wrapped up in sleep. In the faint light of the crescent moon his hair gleamed.

'What exactly are we supposed to do in the graveyard?' I asked.

'Tour it. Prove that ghosts do not exist.'

We plunged on, down the stone path, past the mournful pond, crunching along the gravel through pine trees towards the dreaded gloom.

'Thirty years ago I went on such a tour with a student at this school who is now one of your prominent nationalist politicians,' he said.

'Why?'

'It was just after the Second World War. Two local Africans killed in the fighting in East Africa were buried in the cemetery. The condition of their deaths was grisly and that sparked off fertile rumours. The usual stories, you know – allegations of strange lights seen in the cemetery, soon after the burial, armed figures glimpsed among the tombstones, strange noises – the usual crap, you know. This student claimed to have witnessed these visitations.'

'Did anybody else claim to have seen them?'

'Yes. A local exorcist was even called to quell these so-called disturbances. Afterwards a local priest tried to exorcise the place too. I went on a tour with this student before the exorcisms and saw and heard absolutely nothing.'

'So you think the claims were unfounded?' I asked with a low voice that did not discourage Mr Melbury one wee bit from shouting.

'Absolutely. It was all imagined, and that's what I told this student.'

I didn't like that. I felt Mr Melbury was using me to prove a theory. It was not impossible that he saw himself as a David Livingstone out to deal one final blow to the ogre called superstition. The idea smacked of a paternalism I disliked. In the graveyard, the tombstones gleamed startlingly. It was a large cemetery, some two or three acres bound in by large, mournful *muunga* trees. There was not a single light in that dark expanse. Had I been in a frivolous mood I might have imagined the restless spirits had fled from Mr Melbury himself. Here and there massive crosses towered over smaller ones, Christian crosses defending from fire and brimstone men and women who had lived other lives. The newer tombs dazzled with a stunning sheet-white light, others brooded with a grey blending almost perfectly with the night. The only smell detectable was that of cold concrete, earth and weeds. Dappling that deadland were large tracts of grass, but I knew there were rest houses here too, obliviously scattered, overgrown by weeds and marked only by an old pot or some domestic utensil used desperately to maintain a last link with the living world.

It was these small, obscure graves, shrouded in mystery by their insignificance, which awed me.

Mr Melbury walked up the path, brushing two crosses, and found himself a large bed of concrete to sit on.

'Aren't you coming in?'

'No.'

'Are you superstitious?'

'No.'

'Have you noticed anything or heard anything suspicious so far?' He cocked his ears about him and glanced quizzically back at me.

The silence made me uncomfortable. If a bat had shrieked or a cricket shrilled it might have helped to dispel the obviousness of where we were. All I could hear was Mr Melbury's laboured breath from ten paces away and the heel of his shoe clonking drily against concrete.

He rose up and began his inspection. Every now and then he would stoop to brush leaves off a bed, trace the edge of a stone with a finger, pick up an old pot and put it straight. I began to wonder if he was impressing me or playing the accustomed role of grave attendant.

I felt something wash over my sandalled feet. Ants! Swarms and swarms of tiny ants crawling over me. I was standing on ant's nest. I frantically beat my feet and stamped them.

'Anything wrong?' Mr Melbury enquired.

'Just ants,' I told him, suppressing the urge to scream.

Once, when I was eight years old, I had visited an uncle who lived in the country. While I was there, I was given the responsibility of shutting in the calves every evening. One evening I had chased a reluctant calf round and round the pen. Each time I managed to get the calf close to the entrance of the pen it frisked off into the bushes. It was getting dark. I knew there was an old grave near the pen; one of those now-rare traditional structures of wood and grass placed behind homesteads, next to the kraals. In my frenzied pursuit of the calf I had plunged unaware on to the grave, my arms and legs tripping over the wooden framework. The old grass thatch had caved in on me and my head had ploughed into the mound of sand. I had an unforgettable feeling of being sucked into the sand. With a yell I had torn out of that broken gave, spitting bits of grass out of my mouth, and bolted home. For months I had lived with the feeling of that mouldy sand clinging to my skin. And now, watching Mr Melbury hunched over the tombstone, like a craftsman deeply absorbed in his work, I cursed myself for agreeing to come on this weird tour. My ears began to drum with fear. I was afraid of him.

'Mr Melbury – '

'Yes,' he answered with a triumphant sneer.

'Can we go now?'

'Getting afraid now?' He cackled.

'I don't care what you'll think or say about this,' I told him firmly. 'I don't see the point of this excursion. I'd like to go back now.'

He straightened with surprise and stood for a moment dwarfed among the tombstones. Then he slowly climbed up to me.

I sat in his library while he made the tea. It must have been after one o'clock in the morning.

There were thousands and thousands of books in the room – every bit of wall was covered by books. Most of the books were in hardback or leather casing and were arranged according to authors – Dickens, Shakespeare, Hugo, Lawrence, Austen, Hardy, Conrad and other classics. There were history books and geography books too, natural science, magazines, journals. The room could have passed for a city library. I was impressed by the collection.

'I never lend my books to people, unfortunately,' Mr Melbury said, bringing the steaming mugs of tea and easing himself into a rocking chair.

The presumptuous tone of that statement sent the bile shooting up my throat. Of course I had no intention of borrowing his books, let alone browsing through them. I knew him well enough, now.

'It took me a lifetime to build this collection,' he continued, rocking in his chair. 'You are no doubt wondering what will happen to these books when I die.'

The mention of death made me straighten, with that twinge of guilt young people feel when old people talk about dying. I made a melodramatic attempt to relax but he had already sensed my alarm.

'I'm leaving the books to the school library,' he announced, 'I've already donated two thousand volumes and am handing these over before I leave.'

'Oh, are you leaving?'

'I'm returning to England this Christmas.'

'But aren't you staying on to see this country independent, Mr Melbury?' I ventured.

'That has been my wish for the past forty years. But I'm an old man now.'

I didn't believe that he could concede so easily to old age. I believed he was 'chickening' out, like so many of his kindred who had spent decades in Rhodesia claiming to be liberals but up whose spines the approaching day now sent a chill. I was enraged to think he too had fallen victim to the vision of the holocaust conjured up by malicious prophets of doom.

'Home is home,' he said. Then he fetched his portrait, which I was exploring, from the mantelpiece, and doled it to me. 'You can look at it, of course.'

He looked out of the frame with the same twinkling eyes, the beaked nose and the half wrenched mouth. His head was covered with silver hair, brushed back for the occasion. His ears stuck out sadly from the sides of his head. I guessed he was thirty or forty when the picture was taken, but already there was something trapped in his appearance, a shadow of despair.

'That was the year I joined this school,' he explained. 'Taking or keeping photographs is not my hobby, but I can take pictures of you if you like. I have a camera.'

He fetched a small camera from the rack on the wall. From the way he handled the camera I could see it, too, was a prized possession.

'Not tonight, of course. It's not bright enough. Some other time.'

I finished my tea. I knew he wanted us to talk. There were the books, for instance. There was his life. There was the history of the school. There was me. But I told him I had to go.

'Oh, very well.'

'Thanks for the walk, anyway,' I grinned.

'You can always pop in for a cup of tea and a chat. In the few weeks left away.'

I searched for signs of his surprise at my sudden departure. I liked to think he wanted me to stay longer, until he dismissed me. I felt a little sorry to leave like that but it was good to leave. He opened the door for me and saw me out. He watched me clatter down the stone path towards the grove. When I turned he was still standing in the doorway of that sprawling house, his figure etched in the dim light. I wondered what he would do. Make himself another pot of tea? Read a book? Rock on in his chair? Go to bed?

My head was full of unanswered questions about his life. I was assailed by a multitude of doubts and misgivings about my behaviour towards him. But, said a voice from within me, had I been under any obligation to prove anything? A sudden thought struck me – he wanted friendship. I didn't like the way he doled out every gesture of friendliness. Maybe that was old age but I thought he was too overbearing, his manner too quizzical, for my liking.

I opened the door of the dormitory and glided to my bed. The other boys were asleep. The stale stink of sleep struck me like a plague. The snoring from the beds, arranged symmetrically like graves, was hideous. There was my bed, white and grey, waiting for me. It was two in the morning and the night hung stiff at the windows.

Yes, I told myself as I undressed and climbed into bed, maybe he wanted friendship. Maybe I would go and have a cup of tea with him before the end of the term, before he left the country. But you have to be careful, said my pride, he could humiliate you again. He can be such a nasty little man you have to watch him . . .

Five years later, two years after Rhodesia, with relative quiet, transformed to Zimbabwe, during those months of painstaking integration and the voluntary outward trickle of the faithless, I met Mr Melbury in the capital.

He was standing on a pavement in First Street, watching men and machines at work on a construction site. His back was turned to me. It was the hunchback that caught my attention, and the inevitable grey suit. He turned and his blue eyes, couched behind thick lenses, landed casually on me. Clutching my briefcase in both hands, I stopped.

'I know you,' he said, a livid tongue frozen between pale yellow lips. He looked me up and down in a frantic effort to remember. His complexion was baked red, by the whipping snow, I supposed, and I imagined the pale face was the mark of a passing cold. There was a trace of amusement in his eyes. I must have looked a little earnest in my suit, though I was taller and bearded now.

'Don't tell me who you are,' he urged, 'I'm trying to put my mind on your name.'

I gave him ten more seconds, then announced, with a playful poke at history, 'Mr Melbury, I presume – '

'Why, I even recognise your voice,' he sputtered, 'I know you were at the mission school. Wasn't it you I . . . Oh yes, I remember!'

'Have you forgotten the essay on *wine*-growing and the voice which could go to great depths? The midnight tour of the graveyard?'

A light washed over his face and he roared out heartily. 'Is it you really? How tall you've grown!'

He told me he had just arrived from England for a short visit. After retiring from the mission school he had returned to London, where he now lived. He had come to see how things were 'going on' in Zimbabwe. He asked me about myself. He was surprised to hear I had already finished with University and worked for a year, among other things teaching and writing.

'Written a book!' He gasped, and I told him it was on the shelves. I

58

told him by the time I came into the mission school I was already well into the first draft. He said he wanted to read the book and that there was a friend of his called Mrs Holden who worked in a bookshop four blocks away and if I went there and autographed a copy she could pay for it and mail it to him.

And so I left him there, gazing at the construction site, as I rushed off to my string of commitments. There he was, a man at peace with his condition and me shuttling across the streets with my ludicrous briefcase, burning my soul up in the name of success.

Three weeks later he wrote to me, through Mrs Holden, from London. He had read my book, he said, and liked it.

It is so fresh and vividly honest I wonder what your next work will be like . . . I pondered over the compliment, remembering the paranoia of waiting for reviews that never came, of dreading the sight of my own work, dull-covered and sunbleached in the window of some unfortunate shop, of doing weekly rounds of the bookshops spying on scarcely dwindling stock, the hollowing act of masquerading as a librarian, tricking shop attendants into making orders for the book −

It reminded me of my early days at the mission school when I used to go out with a young student-friend of mine to his home in the neighbouring countryside. The rhythms of season and work you described transported my mind forty years back. One old woman you described reminded me of 'Ambuya', my student-friend's grandmother, who liked me so much she always took me for granted . . . I closed my eyes and saw Mr Melbury strutting in the sunshine of a savannah scene, a self-made anthropologist, wondered at and pitied and loved. It was dimension in his character I had missed altogether.

I'm surprised you never told me you were writing. I did think there was something distinctive in the prose style in your geography essays. You have chosen a fascinating career but I think you will need to be humble and patient if you intend to live on it . . . I was warming to the letter now, but I kept wondering what he would think of the overwhelming tangle of my commitments, my fantasies about cars and women which were so disparate to my first work. What would he say, if he knew?

Then there was that disturbing incident at the armoury, he rambled on into politics, *I hope the situation does not become volatile. So far you have been doing well as young nation; I could see there is plenty of reconstruction going on. But the world is watching you and incidents like these will tarnish your reputation.*

I could see he had not weaned himself of his belief in the prospect of a bloodbath. It was a long, rambling letter, written by a man with all the time in the world to write letters. Once, before I got caught in the rat race, I had been capable of writing such letters. But I felt there was something missing in his letter, something heightened by the way he pontificated about Zimbabwe. There was nothing to indicate his impressions of his new life in London. There was something he was hiding. I was so sure he was squashed up in some cold, dingy room among hordes of indifferent people and sunless grey skies. Though I remembered him saying 'Home is home' on the night of the tour of the graveyard, I was still not convinced that was enough reason for him to leave a place he had known for four decades.

If you care to write to me at the above address I would be most obliged . . . I pondered with amusement at the Victorian etiquette, wondering why he did not just say, 'Please write to me soon. I'm dying to receive a letter from you.'

I put the letter away. I knew I would have to read it two or three more times before writing a reply. It was one of those letters, pregnant with detail, one has to mull over before replying to. I was convinced now that Mr Melbury and I were finally moving towards some kind of friendship. Several days later, I sat down to write to him. I looked for his letter to review it and to find his address.

I looked everywhere but could not find his letter. Foolishly enough, I had not even copied down the address.

I went to see Mrs Holden, whom I knew had the address, the next afternoon but was told she was on leave and would be back in three weeks. With a little despair, I waited for Mrs Holden's return.

Three weeks later, Mrs Holden looked at me up over her cash register and tucked her grey locks over her ears. She was having a hard time remembering, too, and her eyes fluttered when I told her the purpose of my visit.

'You want Mr Melbury's address,' she said, with a hushed voice. 'Oh, I must tell you about Mr Melbury – '

I rummaged through my chest of drawers, unearthing sheaves of regular threats from estate agents and the power supply company, old

Christmas cards, loose receipts, unfiled certificates, dog-eared photo-graphs, lining up the empty drawers on the wall –

I shook out large bulging envelopes full of strange bits of bureaucracy – copies of my lease to life – birth certificates, blood-group cards, insurance policies, testimonials; university contracts, disused lenses, condoms sweating through khaki wrap, notebooks splattered with half-forgotten addresses, old letters, broken necklaces, stubs of friendships –

I wrenched open the headboard of my bed and dredged it of old magazines, poems brittle as dead leaves, shoebrushes, lost identity cards, clippings of pornography, publishers' rejection slips among twists of underwear –

Then I thought it might be in my suitcase, so I pulled out the suitcase and tipped the contents on the bed. But there was little there besides a few clothes rashly bought and hastily abandoned. I combed the wardrobe, turning out pockets, trying to remember what I had worn that day –

Then I thought yes, it might be in my reading desk and I swept through a new morass of paper, pricking my fingers on loose pins.

Had that midnight walk been some kind of rehearsal and did his soul now tour? Or had he asked to be burnt and spilled over the sea?

I felt a surge of guilt and anger – a hard lump in my throat I could not cough up or swallow. I was amazed at how little I knew about him. My eyes were dry, I knew I would not weep. I looked at the morass on the bed, at the excavation around me and despaired. I felt if I found *it*, I might stumble upon the key to our failed friendship.

I tried to remember what I had been writing then and plunged into my manuscripts. I leafed through pages of painful scrawl to a tattered blue file at the bottom of the drawer –

And there, in the file, tucked between two dismal newspaper reviews of my first novel, were the crisp blue sheaves of Mr Melbury's first and last letter –

DENNIS BRUTUS
Goreé[1]

Bring back the implements of slavery,
manacles, chains, the collar, the gouge,
bring back the instruments of slavery
hang them in the forests of the mind
let their windchimes vibrate
in the tremors of time,
and whisper the phrases of guilt
remorse and compassion:
Goreé, Goreé, send back the chains
that our hearts may break
and our tears be unfrozen
and that the healing may at last begin.

1 Goreé: the island off Senegal which was a centre of the slave trade.

IVAN VLADISLAVIĆ
The Brothers

I
V
A
N

V
L
A
D
I
S
L
A
V
I
Ć

Once in High Hope Province there were two brothers called Blokjan and Oswald. They were farmers. They had a pig farm on the road to Nooitgedacht, not far from City Deep.

One Saturday afternoon the brothers were walked home from the City, chatting and making jokes, when Oswald tripped and kicked up a yam, as the saying goes. No amount of hopping up and down on his good foot would ease the pain he felt in the hurt one, so he sat down on a milestone and took off his shoe.

'I think it's broken,' he said, examining his swollen toe. 'If only I'd worn my boots.'

The brothers had spent the morning in the provincial capital, attending to business, which is why they were wearing their town shoes rather than their sturdy, shovel-nosed boots.

'What good is a shoe if it cannot keep a toe from stubbing?' Oswald asked, and lobbed the shoe into the bushes at the roadside.

'None whatsoever,' Blokjan agreed. 'Your toe looks bad. You won't be able to walk.'

'We are far from Vergenoeg.' This was the name they had given their farm. 'What are we going to do?'

'Don't worry, brother. I shall carry you.'

Blokjan was very strong. At the agricultural shows he was known for tossing the porker further than any other man in the district. Oswald decided to put himself in his brother's hands. He took off his other shoe and threw it into the bushes as well. What good is one shoe to a two-legged man?

Blokjan hefted Oswald over his shoulder like a pocket of soup-greens and set off with a long and steady stride.

Oswald's stomach began to hurt, because Blokjan's stony shoulder was pressing into it; his head began to ache, because it was hanging down behind Blokjan's back and filling up with blood; and his nose began to burn, because it was breathing in clouds of fine dust the colour of chilli powder. But he didn't complain, because that would seem ungrateful. He bit his tongue and looked down at his brother's footprints on the dusty road.

After a while Oswald made an observation: the distance between one print and the next was getting smaller. And soon after that he made a deduction: Blokjan was slowing down. He got slower and slower. At last he was going so slowly that he was almost going backwards, as they say in High Hope Province. Then Oswald said, 'I can't help but notice that you're running out of steam, Blok. What's troubling you?'

'I've got plenty of steam – but I think I've skinned my peaches.'

'Well, there's only one way to find out. Let's stop and take a look.'

'I'll just go as far as the crossorads.'

There was a baobab at the crossroads, and the thought of resting in its shade gave Blokjan courage to go on. They soon reached the place. While Oswald was walking round the tree to see whether it had changed since he was last there, Blokjan sat down on one of its swollen roots to take off his shoes. Blokjan too was wearing his town shoes, which were very narrow and shiny, in the fashion of that time, and this must account for the size of the blisters on his soles. You couldn't have covered one of them with a silver slotsak.

'I told you not to wear socks,' said Oswald, reappearing from behind the trunk. 'It causes friction.'

'This is no time for jokes. I cannot walk on these feet, and we are still far from home. What are we going to do now?'

'Don't worry, brother. My toe is much better. I shall carry you.'

Oswald's toe had stopped throbbing. It had been pointing up at the sky and all the bad blood had drained out of it.

Now Oswald was not as strong as his brother, but he was no weakling either: he usually came second at tossing the porker. Some people said that farming with pigs gave the brothers an unfair advantage. In any case, Oswald heaved Blokjan over his shoulder and set off.

Before long Blokjan began to feel queasy. He was not used to being carried. Also, he had eaten a mixed grill at the New Butchery Eating House, one of City Deep's finest establishments, to sustain him on the journey, and now the different parts of it were flying around in his stomach and mixing themselves up disagreeably.

'Any second now he'll get tired and put me down,' Blokjan thought. But on they went. What Oswald lacked in strength he made up for in determination.

At last Blokjan could contain himself no longer. 'I hate to say it, Os, but I've got to go into the bushes.'

On this stretch of the road to Nooitgedacht there was not a bush in sight, just stubbled mealie-fields and empty veld. But Oswald's ear was close to Blokjan's stomach, which was gurgling like a drain, and so he knew at once what his brother meant, and he put him down smartly.

Blokjan climbed through the barbed-wire fence that ran next to the road and walked off into the distance. Oswald sat down and rested his back against a crooked fence post. Blokjan kept walking and looking back and walking again, until when he looked back he could no longer make out his brother's features. Then he judged that there was a decent distance between them, and he squatted down in the sand.

In fact, he needn't have bothered to go all that way, for Oswald had dozed off as soon as he sat down, and he only woke up again when Blokjan returned and prodded him in the side.

'Where's your shirt?' Oswald asked.

'I had to use it,' Blokjan said with a scowl.

'And your jacket?'

'I'm leaving it behind. What good is a jacket without a shirt?'

'So they say.'

'Come, brother, climb up on my back. I can see you are sleepy, but we must get going. We are still far from home.'

'But what about your blisters?'

'Don't worry about them, they are much better. All this sunshine has dried them out.' So they went on, enduring hardships by sharing them.

Every now and then one or the other would say, 'We still have so far to go. What will become of us?'

Without fail one or the other would reply, 'Don't fret, brother, it's just around the corner. I can carry you.'

And it is certain that by this means they would finally have come home to their farm.

But it happened that a stranger was passing through the district, and the road he was travelling by crossed the road to Nooitgedacht. At the crossroads the stranger stopped to rest in the shade of a baobab tree, and there, in the fork of a fat root, he found a pair of shoes.

The stranger licked his finger and wiped a film of dust from one of the pointed toes. Underneath he found very shiny patent leather.

(His own shoes were down at heel and tied together with string.) He pulled a sock out of one of the shoes and stretched it over his hand. It was slightly damp, and it was green, like spinach, and covered in brightly coloured windmills, but there was not a single hole in it. (His own socks had more potatoes in them than a High Hope stew.)

He was on the point of trying on the shoes when he noticed a set of footprints leading off along the road. 'Why would a man take off a good pair of shoes and socks, and go on in his bare feet?' he asked himself. 'I see: someone is playing a trick on me.'

He walked round the tree, but no one was hiding behind the trunk. He walked back the way he had come and looked up into the branches, but no one was concealed up there. He walked on towards his destination, but after a mile he turned round and sneaked back to the crossroads. The shoes were still there.

He tried them on.

He was a very small fellow and the found shoes were much too big for him, but he stuffed the socks into their toes and laced them tightly. They looked wonderful.

'What sort of man would leave behind such a splendid pair of shoes and go barefoot?' he asked himself. 'He must be a fool.' So he turned away from his destination and hurried after the footprints, and as he went he lifted his feet very high so that he would not scratch the leather of his new shoes or kick up yams with their sharp points.

He had not gone far before the footprints veered off the road. A perfectly good jacket was hanging there on a fence-post. He shrugged off his own threadbare blazer, which he had stolen from a truant schoolboy many years before, and tried on the found jacket. There was a bit of peppery sand in the pockets and pigskin patches on the elbows, but otherwise it was in excellent condition. With the sleeves rolled up, it fitted him like a greatcoat. 'He's a bigger fool than I thought,' the stranger muttered and hurried on in pursuit.

For many miles the road ran straight across a flat and barren plain. The stranger saw no trace of his quarry other than the footprints. Once a speck of white in the distance made him quicken his pace, hoping to find a silk handkerchief for his breast pocket, but the speck turned out to be a tattered shirt collar and a pair of cuffs.

At length the road came to a place riven by gorges and cracks and it began to weave in and out among outcrops of rock and boulders piled one on another. Scurrying around one of these piles, the stranger finally caught sight of the man he was chasing. He was just a short way ahead, surprisingly enough, but even more surprising was the monstrous shape of him. He had a huge hump on his back and four arms, two of them hanging down lifelessly behind and two waving wildly about him as he shambled along.

The stranger hurried on fearlessly. When he drew near to the monster he saw that it was in fact one man carrying another on his back.

'Two for the price of one!' the stranger squealed, hitching up the tails of his coat and breaking into a trot.

Blokjan was looking at the ground and counting his footsteps; Oswald, who was tied to Blokjan's back in a sling made from his own jacket, was dozing. The stranger had to dance around them twice and block the way to attract their attention.

'Where did you come from?' Blokjan asked, undoing the sling and letting Oswald slide to the ground.

'I've been following you for many a long mile,' the stranger replied. 'And now I've caught you at last.'

'Doesn't he look a sight,' said Oswald sleepily. They looked at the little man in his huge coat. His coat-tails were dragging in the dust and his long sleeves hung over his hands. You couldn't see his feet either, except for the ends of his shoes sticking out through the folds of his coat.

'Look who's talking,' said the stranger.

Blokjan and Oswald looked at one another. They did look frightful, with their dirty trousers rolled to their knees and their bloody feet bound in the rags they had torn from Oswald's shirt.

'Who are you?' asked the stranger. 'And where are you going?'

'We are brothers and farmers,' said Blokjan. 'And we are trying to get home. But we have been beset by misfortune every step of the way.'

'Who are you?' asked Oswald. 'And why are you following us?'

'I am a stranger in these parts. I have come to tell you that I have a plan, which I am willing to share with you.'

'Go ahead,' said the brothers.

'I can see that you are a burden to one another. My plan is simple:

whoever is weaker should stay here and rest. The other should go on alone and fetch a wagon from the farm.'

'We don't have a wagon,' said Blokjan.

'We have a wagon,' Oswald corrected him, 'but no horses.'

'We had a bakkie once too — '

'A Toyota.'

' — but it was stolen.'

'Ah,' said the stranger. 'In that case I have another plan, a slightly more complicated one, which I am willing to share with you. My good friend Boemke lives near here, and he has wagons and horses aplenty. The weaker of you should stay here. The other should come on with me, to Boemke's, to make the arrangements.'

'We need time to discuss this plan,' said Oswald. 'Please leave us alone.'

The stranger went behind a rock.

'What do you think, Blok?'

'I think it is a good plan, but one thing about it bothers me: why can't he go on alone to Boemke's for the wagon?'

'Perhaps he wants company on the road.'

'You could be right, brother. What do you think of the plan, Os?'

'I think it is a good plan, but there is one thing that bothers me: if he's a stranger in these parts, as he says, how come he knows this fellow Boemke?'

'Perhaps he knows him from way back when.'

'You could be right, brother.'

They were both lost in thought for a few moments.

Then Blokjan said, 'We are still far away from home.'

Amd Oswald replied, 'Don't worry, I can carry you brother, if I have to . . . but it would surely be easier in Boemke's wagon.'

They called the little man out from behind the rock and gave him their decision.

'Let's shake on it,' said Blokjan. He clasped the stranger's sticky claw, Oswald wrapped their hands in both his own, and the brothers shook their hands slowly up and down and intoned, 'What's done is done.'

The stranger looked at them glumly.

'You must also say it,' said Oswald.

'Why?'

'That's how we do it around here.'

'Why?'

'I don't know!' Oswald looked helplessly at Blokjan.

'Because if you don't say it too, it doesn't count,' said Blokjan patiently.

'Very well.'

Their hands were still in a knot between them. They moved the knot up and down.

Oswald said, 'One . . . two . . . three.'

They all said, 'What's done is done.'

'Let's be going then,' the stranger continued at once, disentangling his fingers. 'Who is the weaker?'

'He is,' said Blokjan.

'He is,' said Oswald.

'Your concern for one another is commendable, brother-farmers. But one of you must be stronger than the other. It's only natural. If we had a porker with us, we could decide the issue in a jiffy.'

So it was agreed that Oswald would remain behind while Blokjan went on with the stranger.

It happened that they had stopped on the edge of the Valley of Disenchantment, through which they would have to pass to reach salvation. For most of its course the valley road was lost among boulders and bushes, but on the opposite cliff was one bright ribbon of sand through a clump of aloes. Blokjan pointed this spot out to his brother, and said, 'You'll see the two of us when we reach there, and then you'll know that we are through the worst, and we will soon be back for you.'

'You'll wave?'

'We'll wave.'

Oswald made himself comfortable on a shady ledge. Blokjan and the stranger went down the road into the valley and were lost to sight.

They had not gone far when the stranger, who was walking behind, called out, 'I hate to be a nuisance, fellow-traveller, but I've gone and skinned my plums.'

'You mean your peaches,' said Blokjan.

'Peaches, plums, what does it matter?' He sat down on the ground and took off the shoes. Then he pulled out the socks from the toes. 'These shoes are much too big for me. Why don't you try them on? They look about your size.'

Blokjan unwrapped the rags from his feet and put on the shoes. 'They're a little tight.'

'Better a tight shoe than no shoe at all,' the stranger said ruefully, sticking out his bare feet.

'So they say.'

The stranger's feet were small and pale. 'How will we go on?' he asked. 'My feet are much too soft to endure these sharp stones.'

'Don't worry, stranger. I'll carry you. There's not much of you, as far as I can see, and my shoulders are broad.'

'That's very kind of you. But you've sweated so much your muscles are like river-stones. What if I slip off and fall? Put on this coat of mine, then I'll hold on tight to the cloth.'

Blokjan put on the jacket. 'It fits me well,' he said, 'but it does seem odd without a shirt.'

'Better half a suit than stark naked,' the stranger said, twisting his skinny body from side to side.

'So they say.'

Blokjan picked the little man up and laid him across his shoulders. He was surprised at how heavy he was and how sharp his bones were. The small body pressed into his flesh like an ill-made yoke. But Blokjan was proud of his strength. He began to walk.

The stranger curled his limbs and snuggled himself in. He shut his eyes, the better to feel the swaying of the body beneath him. The tang of its sweat tickled his nostrils, he even thought he heard the surging of its blood.

Blokjan went down into the valley. The little man grew heavier and heavier, but Blokjan kept walking. The little man grew heavier at every step. Blokjan wanted to speak. He wanted to say, 'I can go no further,' and hear the little man answer, 'Don't worry brother, we are nearly home. I can carry you.' But these words caught in his throat, which the stranger's arm encircled like a vine.

They came to the River of Tears in the depths of the valley. Blokjan wanted to stop, to shrug off his burden and plunge his tired body in the salty water. But the stranger was part of him now, cleaving like a lumpy callus to his neck and shoulders. A hot tongue licked at his back and drove him on across the drift. His shiny shoes rattled on the cool stones, the water swirled, then he was on the road again, climbing up between red rocks and dusty bushes.

IVAN VLADISLAVIĆ

Oswald looked out across the valley, to the ribbon of road on the opposite cliff, until his eyes ached. At last Blokjan appeared, dragging his feet and bent over double. The stranger was nowhere to be seen. Oswald started to his feet, calling his brother's name and waving, but all to no avail.

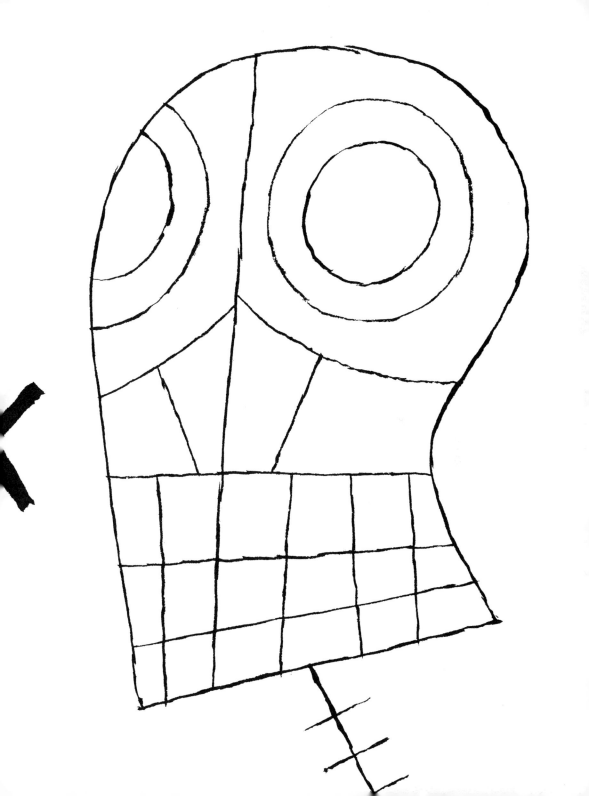

ARTHUR I. LUVAI
Silent Watcher at Sea

Adrift
Leaf and fruit
Of coconut palm
Bob: up-and-down
Over each recurrent wave

Silent on beach
The watcher shakes head
Unable to determine progress to or from
Land or sea . . .

Yesterevening
We swam against the current
Away from the land.

This dawn of undivined promises
We swim with the current
Away from the land . . .

Silent
The watcher stares
At each leaf and fruit
By retreating sea
On beach sand abandoned.

Confusion reigns.

Unable to determine
Progress fromto sealand
The watcher at sea awaits
Our sunset swim.

SILAS OBADIAH
When Tomorrow Is Too Far

Yagana had just finished her evening meal. Her back resting against a kitchen wall, she sat on a stool watching her son Sule polish, with his little fingers, the bowl he had just eaten from. Suddenly there was a knock on the compound gate.

At first she ignored it. Was it perhaps the evening wind playing its usual tricks? When the tap grew louder, she knew that someone was at the entrance. It must be her friend Rupa, she thought, and cooed half-jokingly in her honey-toned voice, 'Break the gate and come in.' She made no attempt to open it. She did not even rise when the knock was repeated with greater intensity. Then her husband Shagiya's groggy voice roared, 'Let me in at once.' Yagana trembled. Only when he was drunk did he sound that husky. Yagana whispered to Sule, 'The beast has returned early from its haunt today.' She expected Sule, who was already on the verge of tears, to burst out laughing. But then the persistent knocking would not let her hear even her own voice. 'Yagana, open the gate. Do you want me to die?' Yagana ran into the sitting room. The food she had put on the table for her husband was in proper order. She came out and prodded Sule, his face streaked with tears, to let his father in. He shook his head in sullen refusal.

Standing in the middle of the compound, Yagana watched as the door threatened to give way under Shagiya's persistent blows. Her small arms were still unfolded across her unevenly large breasts. She began to walk towards the wooden entrance, her heart thumping. Her hands trembled. She recalled other times she had opened the gate for her husband and a fight had ensued there and then. About a month before, such a fight had resulted in a miscarriage, a thing for which she would never forgive him. Another fight almost guaranteed a beating, and her mother-in-law, who often stepped in to stop such fights, was ill.

Once more, she urged Sule to let his father in. Trembling, Sule moved towards the doorway, still crying. As though performing a sacred ritual, he unlatched the gate. It groaned open.

With apprehension Yagana watched her husband stride into the compound. The evening sun cast enough light on him to reveal his stained clothes and bloated face. His eyes were red as those of a hungry lioness waiting long hours for her prey. He walked heavily. The crunching sound of his boots on the pebbles made the chickens cluck, and the goats prick up their leaf-shaped ears. Halfway into the compound, she greeted him. He ignored her completely, stroked his long beard down to his navel and walked into the living room.

She followed him into the house, and found him seated on the usual stool. The room was small with two old wooden stools by the wall. The house had an unusually high mud-coloured ceiling that leaked whenever it rained. In the middle of the room was a table on which lay her husband's evening meal. She moved the table closer to him and sat down on the stool opposite. The light coming through the crevices in the walls of the room was too weak for her to see clearly. She stood up and pushed open the window behind her. Lazy rays of the evening sun spilled into the room.

Shagiya's eyes blinked twice. He removed his shoes, shoved them under the table and washed his hands in a bowl of water. His right hand made to lift open the lid of the dish when he seemed to change his mind. Without raising his eyes from the floor, he snarled at her to open it. Yagana rose gently from the stool and lifted the lid and placed it on the table. He began to eat rather slowly. The look of absent-mindedness which had first attracted her to him crept into his face and she felt elated. It was as if the gentle spirit of his former self had come to visit his face. Now he was the human being he supposedly was.

As though at a sudden stab of pain, Shagiya stared at her and, holding his pointed beard with his left hand, beat his chest violently and moaned, 'I return home and my wife will not open the door for me. What if this small boy were not living with us to do so?' He pointed at Sule, who was just emerging from the bedroom. He went back to his food. This time, he began to chew noisily like a rusty automobile engine. His sound and the stench of *buruktu* beer irritated her, it seemed, to the point of madness. This was the smell of the gutter he sometimes lay in. She would have gone out of the room but for his habitual insistence that she sit before him while he ate. Thus she remained and endured the stench. Covertly, she started at him from the tail of her eye, wondering if he would complain of too much salt in the food as he usually did – an accusation which he could adroitly weave into a quarrel. But he was calm and seemed to like the food.

Just as she began to think that today would be a fight-free day, her eyes met his glaring at her. She ached to see what he was going to say. The red eyes, the foaming mouth, the beard, reminded her of the he-goat that Shagiya had sometimes accused her of sleeping with. This he had said after she had taken refuge in the goat shed to avoid being beaten.

But she had not put any drinking water on the table. She stood up and started towards the door. But, stretching his hand, he blocked her way. Pushing her back to the stool he growled, 'I have asked you a question. Answer me before doing anything else.'

'Don't touch me,' she cried out as she stumbled back on a heap of old books.

A sickly, puppy-like voice chirped from the adjoining room: 'Let me have peace in this compound this evening.' It was Shagiya's mother's customary way of appealing to her son not to abuse his wife.

'Mother,' Shagiya wailed, 'how can there be peace in this compound when my wife will not obey me, when she will not . . .'

'Mother, I was on my way to bring him . . .'

Shagiya lurched towards her and covered her face with a cupped hand. 'If you want to make use of this small mouth of yours again, then you must listen when the head of the house speaks,' he screamed.

'And who is not its head?' she scowled, pushing away his smelly hands. A surprised stare met her eyes. For years she had abided by her mother's instruction not to talk back to him. But this silence had never saved her from the onslaught of her drunken husband.

His mouth hung ajar like a door a thief has just escaped from. As Shagiya stared on, his ant-hill nose began to perspire. Many a time after their fights she had run back to her parents. But they had sent her back with the same insistent words of encouragement: that given time, the man was sure to change. There is no light so long that will not give way to the light of day. She should not run out of patience, her father said, like the restless child in the folktale who left home in search of meat just when a goat was about to be slaughtered. In consideration for her parents, who were too poor to return Shagiya's cow dowry which Shagiya claimed by then would have multiplied to a large herd of cattle, with the patience of a donkey she had often returned and borne all. Remembering the words that poured from the revered lips of her mother, she sat back now and watched Shagiya.

Nodding his head like a lizard fallen from a great height, he fell back into the chair and an expression of pain settled on his face. Then, as if to ease the pain, he held his famous one ear in his right palm. The left one he had lost to his first wife who, sick of a life of brutality, had cut it off and escaped. He began to cough, a hard dry cough that announced the arrival of vomit. She shut her eyes, expecting it.

Finally it came in fierce spurts, gurgling with a rush out of his mouth. Splashing on the table and on the food, it spread generously on the table before finally reaching the edges. Then it trickled in patient drops to the uncemented floor, soaked into it and left there a shiny red substance for her to clean. The smells multiplied. The whole gave off a rich stench: first of a new-born puppy drying by the fireplace, and then of a decayed corpse. The smell awakened in her the memories of other times when she would place a tender hand on him while he vomited in the hope that he would change. This time she was too revolted to do so. She suppressed the surge of pity that arose in her mind and merely stared at him. And as she did, she reflected on her situation.

Her story since her second marriage was that of a woman who had spent a considerable period of her life tending this man who went out every Sunday evening, drank himself helpless, and lay on the floor of the shop of his co-workers in the marketplace cursing and vomiting. Then they rolled him outside and even spat on him. She had to go to the marketplace to search for him and bring him home amidst the mockery of the village children who trailed after him calling him all sorts of names. After she had brought him home, she had to fight for her own survival as he found fault with her. She had to put up with the awful stench that was now a permanent part of the room. She was becoming skinnier every day, and she looked far older than her agemates. Her hair was already greying and her face, grooved with scars, had developed large wrinkles. She was often asked by her workmates who knew her during the happy days of her first marriage or during her school days, 'Yagana, where is that sweet laughter of yours? Why is your face looking so sad like that of a visitor to a place of death?'

What bothered her now as she thought about this was not her

present condition. It was rather her mother's reaction to her situation whenever she returned to her with a swollen face, swearing not to go back. Why did her mother always insist on her going back to the lion's den to live with this knife before her very eyes? Did she want to see mushrooms sprout from her head before she knew that she was indeed dying? Why did she insist on the vain philosophy that her responsibility as a wife implied complete submission? She peered at the future and felt that this hungry knife was always going to be there. Her life was a constant reminder of the depressing side of human existence; of a path of tears without a glimpse of destination. At that moment, the voice of Rupa invaded her thoughts.

Rupa was a friend with whom she had scrubbed floors in the Jengre Seventh-Day Adventist Primary School. She lived not far away from their house with two children – the product of a marriage that had ended in a fiasco. She had never tired of telling Yagana to show the husband that marriage was not a passport to death. She claimed that she herself had gone through a similar situation and patience had failed to do the desired magic. She could only end her ordeal with a fight in which she had almost killed the husband. 'You queen of fools,' she would address Yagana as she watched her wash the stained clothes of her husband in the Jengre village stream. The other women kept a good distance from her and occasionally jeered at her. Rupa listened to her complaints only to chide her: 'If your parents see you as a sacrificial lamb must you help them do so? It is the silence of the camel that readily qualifies it for a beast of burden. Never be fooled by anyone, my dear. In this world of iron, the sword is the best answer to the sword.' Rupa pulled hard at the two long hairs on her chin to emphasise the importance of every word. 'Look, tame that beast you call a husband.' The village women often listened to such admonitions and nodded their heads in approval.

With her head squeezed between her hands, she pondered over Rupa's words of advice. The thought of taming her hsuband in order to 'fly free' had been drumming in her mind for quite some time. It had been coming like madness. Even as she stared at the mirror and saw the sad wrinkles of a discontented cat, she had often banished the thought. First, she considered her small size as opposed to the massive size of Shagiya. If she did, what would she tell her mother whose life's joy depended on how loyal her daughters were to their husbands? But this thought, which had always come in the darkness of the night or her dreams, now came to her with a special momentum. It gripped her strongly. By the time it let her free, she had made up her mind. She would challenge him and avenge herself before she got killed. She would fight him and be killed and her corpse would be carried home to her mother. A childlike excitement invaded her as she thought about being murdered. Her face glowed with happiness and some of its youth and beauty returned to it. Yes, death would end her painful existence. Yes, it would scare her mother and make her spend the rest of her life in grief. And it would certainly teach her a lesson to treat her other daughters more fairly.

She swore by the only nose on her son's face that she would not wipe the vomit. That could be a nice beginning.

Shagiya, who had been bent, stood up with a jerk and shambled out of the room holding the wall for support. Yagana also stood up, glanced at the vomit and dabbed sweat from her brow with the edge of her wrapper. She went out of the room and was greeted by the refreshing air. Inhaling gulps of it, she walked slowly towards the barn and rested her back on its wall. From that position she clearly saw Shagiya sitting in front of his mother's room on a tear-shaped stone. His head was propped between his two hands as if he wanted to prevent it from breaking. He let his head free and tried to wipe his smeared beard. Then he stretched his mouth wide open and closed it. Had a dog done this, thought Yagana, one would have thought it was going to bark. She watched him as he allowed his gaze to dwell on his surroundings. His eyes passed first the goat pen, then the chickens and then further away the kitchen, and then the barn. Then they caught sight of her. Surprise flooded his face, creating ripples of wrinkles on his large forehead. He stared hard at her and holding his beard said in a pretended calm voice, 'Have you cleaned the vomit?'

She ignored the question and then as an afterthought asked, 'What vomit?'

Like a criminal on whom a death sentence is about to be pronounced, he looked down. He sauntered towards the room. Raising the door blind he turned to stare at Yagana. On his face now gleamed a smile more savage than fury. He folded the cuffs of his trousers and yowled, pointing at her with his hook-like index finger, 'If you want this compound to retain the two of us, then go in and mop it.' With a sinister air he moved towards her. Yagana stood firm looking at him. Suddenly he veered round to the compound threshold and pushing the wooden frame closed, locked it carefully and pocketed the key. She ran and shut the door of their bedroom, where he kept the long knife which he would brandish before her, threatening to slash off her dangling dog breasts, as he called them in moments of anger.

She stood looking at him.

'Go in and clean that thing,' he warned.

She walked backwards, looking back occasionally to avoid colliding with the wall that barred her way. Large veins stood out on his face. When he had moved close enough to her, he flung out his right hand to catch her. But having quickened her pace, she escaped his paw. Getting caught in his crocodile-rough hands would be the end of it. Swiftly she turned and raced towards the barn. She reached the far end of the wall that marked the boundary of the compound, then ran towards the barn, keeping an alert eye on him. Just at the moment when she looked ahead to make sure that nothing blocked her way, he increased his pace and pushed her hard on the chest. She staggered and fell. Now he flung his massive weight on her. But she shot out her legs, caught him in the chest and sent him staggering backwards. He fell on his buttocks. Yagana struggled to her feet.

Shagiya's mother must have heard the sound of the fall. But assuming that it was Yagana who had fallen, she begged Shagiya to stop the fight.

Alert with fury, Shagiya looked tough and dangerous as a polished spear. Never before had she seen his chest heaving up and down with such force. If a wild boar had opened up its terrible jaws to swallow her, she could not have been more unnerved. To submit to the butcher's knife, she thought, was perhaps less painful than taking the butcher head on. She wished for a moment that she had obeyed her mother and never lifted her finger to touch or talk back to him.

'Shagiya,' interrupted his bedridden mother in a barely audible voice, 'please, my son, let her alone. She will clean it.' But the appeal only seemed to inflame his anger. He looked towards his mother's room and tried to say something. His beard only quivered with rage.

And so he pursued her. She could hear his feet pounding behind her. She could hear his noisy breathing. He stopped and peeled off his shirt, drenched in sweat. She knew that if she kept him running, his drunken legs would soon get tired and he would have to give up.

But the removal of the shirt was a warning that he was not willing to give up yet. Even Sule, who had been running round the compound crying, seemed to realise this. He cried louder, saying, 'Father, please, don't kill her.'

The goats and the chickens were scattered in the compound. It was as if they too participated in the fight. She was about to turn and run into the kitchen for shelter when a goat blocked her way. Shagiya fell on her. His acid breath came in spasms, seeming to scorch her. His beard, moustache and bushy eyebrows pricked her in the face. Now she knew that he would start pounding her face until she cried out for mercy. Then he would remove her head tie and her wrapper and leave her naked, helplessly crying. She wanted to cry out and tell him that it was Rupa the divorcee who had misguided her. But she did not want to hear her own voice pleading for mercy. She did not want little Sule, who was now crying at the top of his voice, 'He has killed mother, father has killed mother,' to hear her pleading. Just then Shagiya, pressing her head down with his large bony forehead, stretched out his hand to push Sule away. She felt his one ear on her face. Mustering all her strength, she dug her teeth into it. He roared out in pain and let her go. But no sooner had she started to run than he bounded towards her, wiping the blood that flowed copiously from his ear. She had no strength left to shout for help. Besides, the gate was locked, so even if she could shout, anyone would find it hard to enter. 'But I must keep running,' she said to herself.

She recalled the method which Rupa told her she had used to subdue the husband. Rupa would whisper to any woman who dared to fight any bearded husband: once you grab his beard, the man is surely under your control. She slowed down, turned swiftly and raised her hands as if she wanted to surrender. Shagiya staggered to a halt. Before he knew what was happening, his startled beard was in her hand. She pulled it hard toward the hard ground. He grunted, 'Mother, she has killed me,' and fell on his face.

She stood, arms akimbo, her lungs panting like those of a dog and expected him to rise and continue with the fight and kill her. He neither moved nor made any sound again. Slowly she dragged herself to the foot of the barn and slumped down into a heap. A darkness crept over her, the darkness of a sealed tomb. Emerging out of unconsciousness, she groaned with the stabbing pain that racked her body. Around her she could hear familiar voices. Familiar faces were crowded over Shagiya. They poured water on him. Already his mother, who had dragged her sickly figure to the scene, was crying over his motionless form. Not far away from Yagana was Sule. Though alarmed, he was looking at her with a new type of respect. On her tired shoulder she felt a warm hand – a hand with enough warmth to hatch an egg. She looked up and saw who it was. It was Rupa, greeting her with a silent smile. At the sight of her a sudden rush of relief spread all over her body.

MADLINYOKA NTANZI
Praise Poem to Nelson Mandela

*The following izibongo was performed in Zulu by Madlinyoka Ntzanzi
at the African National Congress 48th Congress Rally, Kings Park
Stadium, Durban, 7 July, 1991.*[1]

Power! (To the people!)
Power! (To the people!)
Come Back! (Africa!)
Africa! (Our Land!)

The horned viper with the feathered head
Roared at Robben Island
It roared at Botha's house
So that he had diarrhoea
And left his post.

Botha, who left Pretoria at midnight
Said: 'I am leaving the throne
Take it De Klerk, I have failed.'

The horned viper that roared and South Africa shook
As I listened Ulundi shook
As I listened traitors shivered
They followed saying they want to irritate it
Saying, try to stop it
Saying, it is a Xhosa
Saying, it is not allowed to enter Zululand.

The horned viper that flapped its wings in Pretoria
De Klerk shivered

And said: 'No, take it Mandela
Come and enter Pretoria.'

The horned viper that beat its wings
It came out and went to America
They said it will never enter America
Bush will expel it
It entered and Bush shivered, he said:
'I am welcoming you Mandela,
Enter man.'

When I listened they pointed at it in Britain
Where it saw and spoke to Margaret Thatcher
Margaret Thatcher entered at the wrong place
And left her post.

The horned viper that flapped its wings in foreign countries
They said small dogs tried to follow
It seemed they were attacked by fierce army ants
That were embarrassed in America.

The horned viper that entered the Soviet Union
Where I saw Gorbachev running and following it
Laying down for it a red carpet
He went out to meet it saying the freedom fighter from
    South Africa has entered
When De Klerk tried to run
Trying to go to foreign countries
They kicked him with a heel.

They said, what kind of viper is this, men?
When it beats its wings America shivers
The Soviets shiver
The Hollanders shiver
Britain shivers

The viper is entering, men.

The child of Madiba[2] entered when they said he could not
Coming from the sky, from Johannesburg going to eMpangeni
The betrayers ran to the airport
Trying to stop him
He entered Zululand, men.

He entered, they became confused, saying he has released himself
They slept and woke up wet
They said when they tried hastily to catch him he slipped free
Whereas they are pointing at him inside
I saw him shivering
He said: 'No, I must get out of the way now
The bull will enter, men.'

Even today in KwaZulu the mouths hang wide open
They say: 'Where did Madiba enter?'
Because he entered and said:
'I am going to Ulundi, men.'

Even the intestines of young men boiled
I saw their hot diarrhoea filling the street when Madiba entered
You will see him!

Power! (To the people!)
Power! (To the people!)

1 Recorded by Jurgen Brauniger (Culture and Working Life Project and UND Music Department), translated by Siphiwe Ngwenya (Congress of South African Writers), edited by Steve Kromberg.
2 Madiba: Nelson Mandela.

ZAKES MDA
Blossoms and Butterflies

Blossoms scent the air
And my kinsman
Of the wingless philosophies
He walks
On a carpet of wings
Of butterflies
While daughters and wives
Of revered leaders
Now comatose
Lead us
In a dynastic marathon
To some liberation

Today's pain
Is less harrowing
Than the memory
Of yesterday's
He absorbs the pain
For us all

He sings a sardonic song
As we already know
He sings to ward off kindred spirits
If you take all the moans
In the world
Of sexual ecstasy
And lock them up
In one room
That is his song

A song that lulls the listeners
To a blissful death

In his now famous extensive walks
He comes across
Countless winged worms
They were once butterflies
Wiggling their way
To oblivion

He has won
So he becomes cocky
And arrogant
He wears a blanket woven
From the wings of butterflies

Indeed these are the loneliest moments
Of our life
And the happiest

MANDLA LANGA
Proud Flesh

Umfana wahleka wathi ha ha ha
Is'timela sihambile[1]

It was in the last week of November that the papers reported the case of an Oudtshoorn farmer who had killed a black labourer. The dead man, known as Makgatho, was suspected of stealing a chicken. In a rage, the farmer had bludgeoned him to death. 'It's what these people do,' the farmer said in his defence. He was not going to repent; the kaffir had it coming to him. It was also the week when eight people, five men and three women, were found shot and hacked to death near the KwaMashu railway station. The bodies, in conformity with the universally accepted rule that corpses should be as inelegant as possible, were depersonalised by cameras and eyes that had witnessed their nakedness; they showed signs of torture: cigarette burns and weals caused by sjamboks. Evidently, the beatings, torture and the execution had been committed elsewhere before the bodies were dumped here. There was no apparent motive – there never was – except that all were known to have connections with the ANC. The report accompanying the picture listed the names of the dead, an inventory of horror. Blade read the name of Khaya Ngidi. Something about the name made him sit up from the bed. His mind, befuddled by long nights in the shebeen after playing at the *Crazy Horse* nightclub, was jolted by this discovery. He had known Khaya at Pango where he had been one of the section commanders; then Khaya had left for Lusaka where he had worked with ordnance before disappearing. How is it possible that a trained man like that could have been caught unawares? Blade knew that many such questions would remain unanswered for a long time.

He washed and dressed. When he looked at himself in the mirror, he encountered a stranger. His eyes were bloodshot; there was a bruise above the left eye. What happened? He thought of going to ask Lungi, who was pottering about sullenly in the kitchen. He knew she must be angry because he couldn't remember how he had got back. He imagined people carrying him from the car, depositing him, like a sack of meat rations from a Lusaka butchery, on the front *stoep*, knocking and leaving hastily when the door opened to avoid Lungi's interrogation. She had a sharp tongue, that one, Blade thought, marvelling at her spunk but at the same time sickened by his dependence on her. What has become of us? he wondered.

It was in her eyes that he saw how thoroughly condemned he was. They were puffed and red from crying. This was somehow unlike Lungi, who was as tough as nails; but, he knew, he had penetrated her shell and was able to touch those parts she had protected with her tongue and toughness. *She makes love just like a woman,* he remembered lines from an unforgettable song, *and she breaks just like a little girl.* He came up to her and she turned her back and concentrated on cleaning the stove, the kettle boiling on a side plate, the hiss of the steam filling the kitchen. Somewhere in the house a radio played a song that celebrated passion.

Even the president needs passion, someone sang and Blade remembered a president he had known and respected and would have died for if the opportunity had been there. But that was a long time ago. So much had happened and he knew he had changed and been changed by his re-entry into his country. Tsidi and the chief: what had happened to them? He knew that the chief was still alive; such things can never be kept out of the media. And Nsimbi? Who was his latest poison victim? Who are the victims? He touched Lungi's shoulder, felt the thin silky fabric of her nightgown, and something knotted up inside his stomach.

'I am sorry, Lungi,' he began.

She turned round to face him, the wet face looking as unfamiliar as a stranger's; her eyes searched his in an attempt to come to the bottom of the mystery of what had bonded them together in the first place. He had known how easy it was for lovers to become, at some snarling hour, total strangers. What mystified him was the knowledge that people organised liaisons with the knowledge of the probable moment of parting always at the back of their minds. Or, to be more precise, that was how he approached relationships. This realisation always filled him with sadness because he knew that he was beyond the point of feeling. Throughout life, he had been going through the motions. So, when she turned to look at him like that, with those wounded eyes, he wondered for the first time whether he really didn't hate women.

'Why do you do such things?' Lungi asked. It was a question that came with the ease – and difficulty – of having been repeated over and over until it had become the only question that connected them, that could be the basis of their relationship. 'Do you want to leave?' she asked.

'What day is it?' he asked.

'Friday.' Lungi continued looking at him, possibly trying to find in his face some recognisable pieces which could be glued together to rebuild their shattered lives. 'If you want to leave,' she went on, 'feel free. It's cool with me.'

'What did I do . . . last night?'

'You don't want to know.'

'Seriously. Tell me.'

'Where should I start?' Lungi asked. 'The fight at Nokwe's spot? How you groped Sis Patty and boasted that you're the playboy of the Western world? Or how you were chucked out when you picked a fight with Alf? Or the wet sheets in the hamper? Should I go on?' He shook his head. 'No.' Sighing, feeling that he wouldn't be able to face a single soul outside, he sat down on the kitchen chair and looked at the flies on the lace curtains.

'The problem here,' Lungi said, 'is that people won't know what has happened to you. You know that for many of us a returned exile is something like a king. We look up to them because they have been outside this stinking mess. And they have been fighting. Young people look up to you, their brilliant light. What do you think happens to them when they see a drunk pissing all over himself? Do they feel that all this was worth it?'

'No.'

'Of course not.' Lungi rinsed her hands under the tap. He had an impression she was washing her hands of him. 'And that's the easy part. The harder part is that people are dying here. There's an open season on ANC people, you must just read the papers.'

'I read the paper this morning,' Blade said. 'I guess I know what you mean.'

'Blade,' she said, 'I want you to know that I sincerely thought that we had something good going, but you must have heard that a thousand times already.'

'What do you want me to say?'

'That you'll try and save your life.' She gave him a chilling look

108

and he imagined she saw him lying tortured, naked and dead on the page of a morning newspaper. 'We people who never went into exile – we had to deal with the shit in our neighbourhood. We witnessed teargas and guns and explosions and limbs and guts spattered all over the show. I am not a political person, I never was. But I have eyes that can see – and what I have seen is enough. I am one of those who believed that one day men like you are going to come with guns in hand and help free the country. All of us used to shout, "*Mayibuye!*" with our thumbs stuck out like this.' She made a fist which looked like a child's, and smiled at a grim memory. 'We loved then. We loved the sense of community, the togetherness. Nights blazed and introduced the horror in the morning, but still, we held on to one another, like a whole community of brothers and sisters.

'There was this time, Christmas 1989,' Lungi continued, 'and the children came and told us that Inkatha would be attacking. You see, at G and F and K and E Sections – the people knew that it was a no-go area for Inkatha. They had been beaten even when they came with the ZP's. So, we must have relaxed a bit. But now the children were telling us this story. And most of the men were at work or – as usual – in shebeens, getting drunk.' She wrinkled her small nose, pronounced the last phrase in English: gettin' dronk.

'We knew they would be coming in through *ezimpohlweni* – the hostels. Which meant they would have to cross the railway line between Thembalihle and KwaMashu stations. There was a possibility that they would railroad the residents at B Section, or even pick up some reinforcements at D or C.

'That was when the women, whose grapevine is more effective than all the telephone wires in the city, got together and marched. We walked from here to K and J and L and M, picking up anything that wore a skirt. Everybody. Beauty queens marched with shebeen queens and schoolgirls; teachers, off-duty nurses, domestic workers, people who would be doing night shift, *zonke zothayi*, *kwaba ududulayini*, *ngempela* – and we were singing, Blade. All these women were singing:

Wathint'abafazi
Wathint'imbokodo
Uzokufa![2]

109

And, as she sang, Lungi stamped her foot on the tiled kitchen floor, shimmying, doing the *indlikizane*. Blade, who knew the township mamas, imagined this cloud of angry womanhood. He smiled.

'It's no laughing matter!' Lungi snapped. 'At least, the Inkatha impi wasn't laughing.' But despite herself, she began to giggle. 'Some of the mothers, scared of leaving their sons alone in the house, dressed them in women's clothes and forced them to join the march. And some transvestites, *ongqigili nezitabane*, came out, too, on this day of liberation and added colour to the procession.'

The march leaders called a halt at a spot along the main road running from the township gates to the end of D Section. There was a low bridge which was known as KwaVezunyawo, whose steps leading to the other side were usually covered with dried blood, piss and vomit. It was a notorious spot, hence its inelegant name which conjured images of people who had been robbed and dismembered. The women waited, singing their songs repeatedly; the impi came from the other side, also singing, jazzing themselves up for an orgy of mayhem. They saw the women. The hundreds of marchers sent an ear-splitting ululation, dancing and raising the dust. The police who stood watching – as was their fashion – from a safe distance, diverted traffic, waving delivery vans back. 'The township goes crazy at the sight of a delivery van,' Lungi observed dryly.

'The more daring of the women', she said, 'stepped forward and bared their breasts, singing and taunting the men, telling them that it was because they were not men that they spent all their time killing people. "*Come on*," they shouted, "*come and get us and we'll show you your mamas!*" The men shook their heads and got into a huddle. A helicopter hovered above this confrontation; later, after curses and promises of a bloody end to women's meddling, the men left with their tails – and a lot besides – between their legs, and the singing was considerably less heroic.'

'Was this reported in the papers?' Blade asked.

'Ja,' Lungi said. '*Ilanga Lase Natal* made it look like women were out of their minds, saying that people had been baring their breasts and all that. But some papers, such as the *New African* – which is certainly not Gatsha's favourite paper – managed to invest the whole affair with the appropriate dignity. It had an editorial taking issue with the men who could show more commitment towards the peace process.'

Blade looked at the flies; they still moved slowly, inching up the lace. The sun which came in through the window to wash the aluminium sink and the polished floor; the hum and buzz of the township outside; the voices that entered in snatches: mothers yelling at the children and the children playing: all this became the sight and sound of home. This is where memories begin and this is where they end. He thought about the dead people, a drop in the ocean of corpses that had been piling up since the beginning of *udlame*, the troubles in the country. Looking at Lungi as she made tea, feeling like telling her that he didn't want any since he had a hangover but deciding to do the right thing, something in the way the sun caught the side of her face as she moved reminded him of Thandi. What had happened to the baby? How long was it now?

He had returned to KwaMashu after Groutville and searched the cemeteries for his sister's grave. What hurt to the quick was the revelation from the burial official that, even though there was a grave marked with her name, someone else, a fifteen-year-old girl, was buried there. This knowledge, that he could never really finish the process of mourning without seeing her grave, rocked him. He drank and brawled and played the saxophone with a group of musicians he had known before leaving the country. Blade knew, even in the deepest throes of inebriation, that all this was a futile attempt to forget the unforgettable; he was merely delaying that moment when the tears would flow like a river after heavy rains. When he played, then, he enveloped himself in a shroud where it was possible to remember without pain. The notes that poured out of the saxophone's brass bell, were the unshed tears; they carried in them years of suppressed rage and longing.

He had been shocked, one day, as he walked down Albert Street, when he stumbled into Lungi. They had been at school together oh, so many years ago. What amazed him was that, although the years had taken their toll, she was still Lungi. He had remembered some of the guilty moments when, as an acne-ridden adolescent, he and the other boys had used mirrors to try and look up women's skirts. Lungi had always been a mystery. When the boys indulged in communal masturbation, it was her image which caused him to groan and spill his seed in the urinal.

'I didn't know,' she laughingly told him later when he revealed his earlier fantasies to her, 'that you had such a dirty mind — and fingers! And there we were, the girls, thinking you were such a nice boy!'

'Nice boys are the worst when it comes to those things.'

She had accompanied him to the performances, more out of duty than anything else. Furthermore, it also meant she could keep an eye on him. It was in the way she held him that Blade knew how terrible the beast of loneliness was. He was lonely himself, and this clawed at him in the midnight hour, and caused him to sigh and moan. He felt guilty, when they were making love, when images of Mary or Tsidi flashed before him, clashing like apparitions from a past that refused to be obliterated. Something in him said that this was wrong and indecent. Wrong because, here she was, Lungi, overflowing with an emotion she expressed as love, and he was incapable of reciprocating. Judging himself unselfish, he wrestled with the meaning of surrendering one's personality to another. What was love if there was no give and take? Women had this great capacity to give, and receive nothing; and men the world over strutted on the sidewalks of time with their shoulders braced against the moment when they would be called to settle the account. Because, he knew, someday – a day that soon a-coming – the women would rise up, much like the marchers of KwaMashu, and demand a better deal. What would happen then? Even in the camps, he thought, the language that tried to decipher the hidden codes of gender failed. We spoke of building a new man – and this formulation came as easily as breathing – and we never saw the paradox, the immense irony in it. When women fighters such as Thandi Modise were praised, the comrades would say, *She fought like a man*. Blade would wonder, at moments when he could still think clearly as alcohol burned down his throat, whether the new South Africa would usher in a different impulse; whether men and women would enjoy relationships on a common footing without something unnameable snarling in their midst. He knew that it would be hard since, for him, whatever relationship he had with women was burdened by the baggage of tradition and custom.

His sister: she must have been a woman to those she interacted with. She must have loved and been loved in some panting instance of her life. He tried to imagine her with a lover, wondering whether she, too, had been capable of opening up like a flower and whisper the name of her heart. What she had thought about when she died? Had it been painful?

'You're crying again,' Lungi said. He knew that he had been doing a great deal of crying since the return from the cemetery. He had been woken up by his own choked sobs at night, and Lungi had cradled him, sometimes going as far as singing a lullaby, doing anything that could connect him with a life he once knew so many decades ago.

Because, he felt, what else was left but tears? The township and its rhythms, the children that walked and played and imitated adults at war: what was there for them except a legacy that was as obscene as an open grave? And the people themselves: every day they struggled against insurmountable odds, going into trains that shuddered with them every day to arenas of battle. In the factories and offices and the madams' kitchens, the people would encounter contempt as real and corrosive as desert storms. They would swallow insults from the children of the powerful, their eyes choosing not to see the faces of the parents congealed in distorting hatred. The mamas brought back fruits and vegetables from the markets and the fathers returned with more tales of woe. The evening meal would be a theatre of coded words and inexpressible gestures where the eyes of the children would be watched; because, no matter how irresponsible they might finally be judged, parents are uneasy with terror touching their children.

He remembered one of the first days back in KwaMashu when Lungi and her friend Juliet drove to Entuzuma, a sprawling expanse of township houses which stretched from the hills of KwaMashu to the edges of Inanda. On the way, they found twelve- and thirteen-year-olds filling a rut on the road with earth and stones. The kids stopped the car and their leader, an unsmiling boy who wore a khaki felt hat approached Blade's side.

'We have fixed the road for you,' he said, 'so that your cars can have a smooth ride. Now, *ngicela nisixhase.*'

'What does he mean, *sibaxhase?*'

'He means they want support for their effort,' Juliet said. She seemed uncomfortable with the kids. 'Just give him any coins you have.'

Blade took out a bunch of coins from his pocket and, without counting them, dropped them in the open hands of the boy. He was totally illiterate with the new coins of his country. He couldn't separate the new two-rand coin – called de Klerk – from the twenty-cent ones. What the hell. When they drove off to the salute of the kids, he asked, 'Is this happening a lot?'

113

'You mean kids acting like the Highwayman?' Juliet asked, relieved. 'All the time. At least these didn't threaten to smash the windows or burn the car. Kids have been known to force you out of the car and take it. And there's fuck all you can do about it. This is the future of our country, Blade.'

'And the parents? What do they do?'

'Nothing. The parents themselves are in need of someone who can *xhasa* them.' It was as if Juliet was irritated by the question. 'This is our reality.'

It was this reality – the reality of all the blasphemed days – which forced Blade to start thinking seriously about the meaning of life. He could shed tears but what help was that? There were positions he had taken on violence, telling himself that he would never again carry a weapon, or take a life. But, the images in the newspaper, the shells of men and women that had once supported life: what was to be done to stop all this? He felt the throbbing headache and knew that he was in for a bad day, and this thinking wasn't helping matters much. But he had to think. When the fire blazed in the townships during the States of Emergency, comrades had debated about the use of necklaces on informers. He had been one of the people saying that this practice was wrong; it was barbaric and repellent. The standpoint of other comrades was that the necklace was a necessary method to discourage an exercise that had led to so many deaths, that was causing the struggle to drag longer and longer. 'Look at it this way, *chumza*,' someone pointed out, 'if there were no informers, *izimpimpi*, we'd have long done one thing with the Boers.' But Blade was still convinced that, while it was true that one had to fight fire with fire, the necklace wouldn't bring the liberation day any closer. Killing informers or counter-revolutionaries just meant adopting the patterns that the revolution advocated against. Then there was the time spent fighting Unita, something he could justify, the same way he could wiping out an enemy platoon. But that was different, he told himself, wasn't it? It was war. And now . . . ? These bodies that screamed for some explanation – was this not war? The government in South Africa armed with its state machinery: had it not effectively declared war against its black citizens? It didn't matter that, in the main, the people who did the dirty work were themselves black – they were conscripted troops, handmaidens. Even as he thought, something nagged him. He couldn't shake off the feeling that all this was somehow connected to Nomusa's death. She must have known something about these death squads, professionals who had the uncanny ability to target ANC people. In solving the mystery of her death, Blade knew, he would come closer to the bottom of these killings. Nothing was unconnected.

'What's happening tonight?' Lungi asked.

'We're still playing at the club.' Blade drank the tasteless tea and wondered whether the nausea would rise and he would have to get to the bathroom. 'After this,' he said, 'I'd like to take some time off.' He thought for a minute. 'How much preparation has been made for the conference? Is it still going to be held here in Durban?'

'It will be in Johannesburg,' Lungi corrected him. 'Branches are meeting and people are discussing papers.' She paused and listened to the sounds outside, like someone who had been interrupted while making an announcement. 'Frankly, I wonder how the two Natal delegations are going to manage, what with all this violence!'

The hunchbacked hills and valleys of the land, the rivers and the steady rock, the city and the countryside, all had been touched by the violence. It was there in the packed kombis and bakkies which transported passengers between the city and the township, people squashed into one small dream like so many sardines. It would happen – it had been predetermined by laws of trade and commerce that a taxi can only make money by making as many trips as possible – that a vehicle would veer off the road and crash into an embankment with its screaming cargo. Blood would flow on some of the best roads of the country, trickling into the culverts that had witnessed so many such scenes in silence. The birds that flew above would stop in mid-air and gaze with uncomprehending eyes at the ease with which people died. Or the trains thundering into ruined tracks, the steel and timber splinting together with the bones. The government of the day would declare itself innocent, blacks have this bad habit of dying in the most unexpected places. But the violence that chilled the blood came from the people. They stopped funeral processions and hacked coffins and caused mourners to flee. It was so bad that in some rural areas it was impossible to bury people during the day. The atonal account by a dry-eyed specialist in the necklace: *We really didn't mean to kill him. It sort of . . . happened. You see, he was there, and we had roughed him up a bit, and he already had that expression on his face of someone who had accepted death. We slung the tyre round his neck and poured petrol all over it, inside. And, when he was handed the matchbox and the stick, we told him to light it. I stood there, singing, and I heard the match rasping against the striker. It was a strange sound, something that will live with me for ever. And then, just the whoosh! and green and red and blue flame enveloped him. I turned away when I heard the eyes popping.* There was the case of a comrade who had died in an Inkatha stronghold. His parents were informed in no uncertain terms that his body was not be buried in the region. The people, who could not call upon others to help, carted their unmourned relative to another town where he could be buried in peace. The price of peace was too high. Blade wondered whether the conference would organise for some of these relatives to attend. People needed to hear these testimonies from hell. The question was, who would bear to hear such a tale? For, Blade told himself, this country beats Beirut or Belfast by a long mile; the murders and rapes have earned preternaturally beautiful cities like Cape Town the label of the murder capital of the world. The crack wars raging in Harlem and Washington pale into insignificance in the face of an organised impi armed with traditional weapons which changes the history of a settlement and turns people's lives upside down. And the sun shines in the morning on those whose hands are filled with the blood of the innocent. White men go on making love to their wives and strike their children, and have their bacon and eggs and on Sundays go to the chapel to worship their Saviour, nothing in their eyes communicating what they have sanctioned. The wives in summer frocks and sun bonnets and sunglasses holding on to their charges who, born innocent in a guilty land, already know how to own and command, their eyes not reading the ghastly headlines about people who have been slaughtered on their behalf. The way meat-eaters are at peace with the world after a filling meal of lamb stew. And academics and intellectuals from the university supply statistics and monitor violence in a land where it is a crime to nurse the wounded or give succour to the bereaved. Their findings take them to the capitals of the world where slides are shown and films are made and books are written and reputations established. What madness is this? Have these people ever gone out to look at the sea and the rivers and the azure skies that hover above mountain ranges, stretching in summer as the breeze let the cottony clouds ride like waves? or the trees, some with no name, and the herbs that breathed a pungent scent of healing and strength above the dark upturned earth which is supposed to support, to *xhasa*, all life? or the breathtaking viridian beauty of the Valley of a Thousand Hills? Do they not hear the songs of nature, the symphony of stone and sand and birds that sing even to the springbok in a trap?

But now we all smile, baring the teeth of ceremony. The exiles move from lands that become forgotten as time passes. The women ululate in a wedding or when someone gives birth, the cry no different from the keening wail at the gravesite. The men jump into the nearest beerhall and drink and drown and rise no more. The young ones watch. They see their friends growing up in despair; the young woman with eyes as ageless as the sun knows her body is being watched by wolves. The wolves laugh and slink into corners and blow another blast of Durban Poison and a desperate drunk sings *Swing Low, Sweet Chariot*, wishing for caring human hands to hold him and carry him home. But where is home? Tears sprang into his eyes.

'Why did you come back, then,' Lungi asked, 'if this country gives you so much pain?'

'Why do people return?' Blade countered, knowing that the answer lay somewhere deep within himself. 'Mainly because exile is so intolerable, no matter what people say. And there is always that wish, when you are outside, to taste again the air of the country that brought you up. To find out if all the dreams you had, the images you conjured, are true. I know,' he went on, shaking his head, 'that it sounds silly and coy. But, for most musisicians and writers, exile kills creativity. We moved along, allowing ourselves to be swept by a wave, having no control. Writers had to depend on street maps of their mother country. There was the miserable partying where we told each other how much we would make it in London, how South African creativity had also contributed in humanising the Brits. But the question we hardly asked ourselves was: did the British public need us? We certainly needed them, no matter how we pretended otherwise. And – this was startling – we found out in the loneliness of our flats that we who had intended to change other societies had actually been changed by them. So, who won? I found out, for instance, that I liked my flat, the freedom of being alone on my own terms. I realised I hated any invasion of my space, which is a very British thing. I was every day shedding off the skin of Africanness.

117

But, on a spiritual level, Britain was beginning to make sounds with which I couldn't identify, and all the while I was outside myself watching me in this predicament. Life there was like looking into a mirror whose surface had dulled, leaving a blankness that was quite frightening. I saw myself spending another winter, bleak and grey, with everyone cursing that the sun sets at 4.00 pm. And all of us, in the Underground, locked up like moles, all of us thinking of suicide. I was becoming quite self-destructive.'

'But,' Lungi dug in, 'South Africa hasn't exactly been the elixir of life, has it? For you?'

'My reality has been fucked up for me,' Blade said. 'But still, there's something to claim here, which I couldn't find in Europe.' He tried to shape coherent argument for being back in the country, and then it hit him, like a bolt. 'The bones.'

'What?'

'The bones,' he repeated, gazing into the glass which had now darkened as a cloud passed. The mystified flies held on and then let go. The memory, triggered by something unknown, a quality full of changing and stillness, like a heartbeat, brought it all back. It had been hidden in some deep corner of his mind, waiting like an Easter chicken, to burst out into a new day. 'The bones have always been there, laughing at our stupidity.'

'Maybe,' Lungi advised, 'you should take an aspirin and lie down.' She touched his brow with her palm, the hand feeling cool, like the hand of a stranger one is forced to fear. She shook her head in the fashion of an indiscreet physician encountering a terminal case. 'Whatever it is that's bothering you,' Lungi said, 'just make sure it doesn't kill you in my house.' She attempted a smile but her face contorted into a grimace of pain.

'Do you remember . . .?' he began to say and then stopped himself. Of course, she wouldn't remember. She had seen nothing; he was again confusing her with Tsidi. He was suddenly impatient with her and wanted to get away. But, at the same time, he dreaded going out alone. The weight of the months he had spent in the country came and rested on his shoulders; the longing and the wish to comprehend the workings of the hearts of men and their gods became a living thing that sapped his energy. He was no different from a man with an *ilumbo*, a ravaging disease which confounds the best healers. Making a tremendous effort, he stood up and shuffled into the

bathroom. His eyes accusing him in the unblinking glass, he held on
to the bowl and threw up. The long process left him weaker than
before, the sweat pouring out of him like a stream. When done, he
rinsed his mouth and cleaned up, the vomit reeking of bile, tea and
recycled malt and spirits. He felt empty, like a new vessel.

He woke up later when the Friday evening whispered itself into
his dreams. They had been hard and unattainable, shadows that
danced and reminded him again of the bones. Outside the cars rolled
on, but now with a muted sureness, as if the dark were a cloud that
cushioned everything. Feeling mellow and hungry and hard, he
turned to Lungi who lay awake in companionship of healing and
solidarity, the way people lie next to their ailing compatriots. He
wondered what she had made of his delirious babble, because he
remembered the dreams that had rolled and unfolded in front of him
like pieces from a frustrating puzzle. The voices that had been in his
head; the screams and irreverent laughter: but he could shrug off all
this now. The time to wrestle with personal demons was past and he
felt a great tenderness envelop him with a diaphanous veil.
Somewhere, in the state of sleepy wakefulness, he had cried when he
couldn't find answers to his confusion. In the vignettes that translated
themselves into images, he had experienced a great sadness when he
found that he couldn't blow any more; the mouthpiece of his
saxophone had crumbled like rotting sugarcane and the sound had
been a rasp akin to a death rattle. It was with great relief, then, that
he found himself in the land of the living. He recalled the bile that
had touched his brain, the bitterness he had felt against the people of
his country, how he had condemned them and cast them into the
deepest darkness. He knew – waking up alive and whole and sane
insinuated this – that no matter how crazy things might be, life was
still a gift. It was short and, hence, it had to be cherished. The
misguided sons and daughters of the masters of the land, he told
himself, would one day wake up and their eyes would be opened and
they would see that the promised land was more livable when shared
among the people. Those who held on to national anthems and
monuments and icons which excluded others, would know that a
melody is enhanced by more people singing the same song. The
worship of heroes and generals decorated in obscene wars of
aggression was as obsolete as a pillory, men and women of the world
had to move with the times and sing a song that would bind them

and glorify their common humanity. And the children of the world would understand – this knowledge would be painful but necessary – that paradise is acquired at a price and should never be forfeited, and that love is a bounty which nature bequeaths on the deserving. Where there had been turmoil and turbulence, a calm reigned and Blade Zungu, musician and reluctant returnee, heard himself calling out her name. Then he stretched his hand and touched her on the hip, feeling the heaviness between his legs, something rising like a tide; and he caught the smell of the room, the perfume bottles arrayed on the dressing table – and she murmured and edged closer and stuck her tongue in his ear. Then his fingers, working involuntarily, peeled off the thin blouse she had changed into, and he felt the satiny skin beneath, warm and cool, the rising mound of her breasts, the nipples. He tasted them and rolled each one in his mouth, alternately, mischief guided by a need to discover and savour. The tight braids under his hand, her neck arched, the fingertips stroking the nape, a tender spot. Then the night darkened and the playing ended with the bodies wrestling on the sheets, time suspended, their breath making a statement that has eluded the wisest of men, the flesh speaking in tongues until the release, *yebo!*, *yebo!* and the savage tremors abated and the storm transcended itself into an indelible commemoration of tenderness, the final clenching.

1 The boys laugh, ha ha ha
  The train has gone

2 'You have struck the women
  You have struck a rock
  You will die!'

TOM A. OCHOLA
A Return to African Quarters

Strangers.
Faces frowned.
Twisted eyebrows in hurried headshake.

At the next doorstep
Dirty water is rudely spilt
And the door slams cursingly.

I search the youthful blood
And the warm bonds of my grandmother's hearth —
Beyond the fearsome giant Kakamega Forest
On which the squalid Nandi Escarpment boldly lies;
Now a pale ordinary hue,
Now almost flat.

I venture into the tinlids
Sande hammered on to stickends
Or the skeleton cars forged from copper wires,
Ready for the infantile motor rally;
Or the genius of Ochieng with stringless guitar
Twanging the rhythms of Lucky jazz band,
And Wycliffe with wooden pistols
Playing American cowboy
On invisible horses.

Gone too
Is the dry dry December wind,
Coming into the desolate town
Deserted by holiday makers,
And the dreadful Khalitsa,

At the feet of a shadeless tree,
Blowing cigarette smoke
Through his nose.
I go back to my room.
A cold bed.

I take my jacket
And walk the empty night.

Strange laughter in nightclubs.
Heavy bass droning like a powerless gramophone.
Dull drums thudding sickly . . .

And
      Suddenly
           a flash.
                Large drops drum tinroofs.
                    crash.

Darkness.

In the morning
I pick my pieces
A fruitless homecoming.

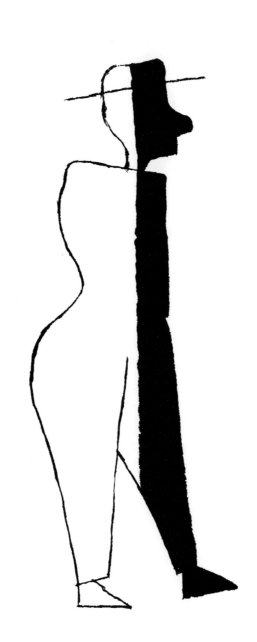

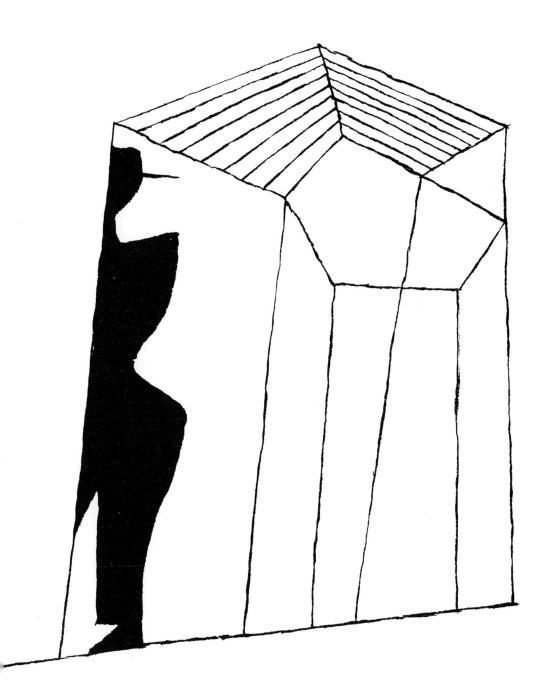

UNGULANI BA KA KHOSA
The Orgy of the Deranged

The senses, like a snake once it had shed its skin, were awakened from that lethargy brought upon by the consciousness of death, predicted early on by the start of the pains. It was night, as he found out later, but at that moment, as if emerging from the abyssal depths of the spirits, the sounds were going inside his body. It was the *chikhulu*, the name given in these lands to the double bass of the marimba, joining the loose pieces of a body broken by pain; it was the *chilanzane*, name given to the soprano, opening the arteries of a river of blood that those who had created the agony had staunched with the apocalyptic certainty of the millennium; it was the *debiinda*, designation of the bass, reactivating the irrigation motor that had been made rusty by the times of anguish, of which there is no memory.

He opened his eyes. He saw the night. The stars. The moon. I see, he thought. He smiled. He twirled his fingers. He buried them in the moist sand. The creeping vegetation grazed against his body. A firefly awoke and threw itself into space, covering the non-existent tracks of all the nights with a senile somnambulism. The owls, in a belated concert of heinous premonitions, chirped in, without the help of a conductor, their senile measures. The *dole*, designation given to the tenor, leapt out of the body and filled the night. He raised himself. The elbows carved small holes in the sand. I feel, he murmured. And he again reclined himself in the position of those who have died. The moon, glutted with the pompous meal of the nocturnal day, let go of the fine threads of the resting hour and smiled on seeing the bands of light trickle beneath the tree trunk in lunar motions. He got up. The soles of the colossal feet planted themselves on the ground. The hands, freed from the sand, allowed the wind to decipher their destiny in the non-existent strokes of hands that had no future. He laughed. The laugh, made into a bubble by the wind that had deciphered nothing, threw itself at the distant rocks, was thrown back by the slope of the tomb-like shadows and returned, weakly, to the glued lips of a broad-shouldered man. He shuddered. The images, flying back in retreat, ran through the mind. Memory had sheltered itself in the cave of his existence.

'Ny name is António Maposse.'

And he cried.

A sound. Various sounds. Smoke. The voices raise themselves, confound each other, disperse, join each other, disappear. The land swings around like a ship going in no direction. Vomited blood covers the floor. The counter is rent wide open. The roof tiles fly like prehistoric birds. The roofs have vanished. The foundations cry out. The doors fall to pieces. The window panes are turned into a dust that reeks of death. The sound grows. The smoke hangs over the sky. The bodies are swaddled by a river of blood. I'm going to die. The hands run through one of the beams of the store. The night envelops the morning. Pieces of flesh are detached from the bodies. Screams. Strange footsteps. Deathly sounds. I'm going to die. Drowsiness comes nearer. It enfolds him. The body wavers. It whirls. Falls. He doesn't hear the fall. Maria! he calls out. His eyes awaken. The sun, red, falls on the horizon, mortally wounded. A strange setting. Maria! . . . The voice low, hoarse, far away. The cockroaches, apprehensive, grope through the floor of blood. Rats lurk in the background. He gets up. His feet scatter the remnants of roof tiles. The eyes search. They see scattered grains of mealie, *capulanas* torn away, nameless corpses, bullet shells, gutted walls, giddy rats, frightened cockroaches, disintegrating walls, blood, blood, Maria! . . . The feet feel their way in the floor of blood, stumble over rafters, trample mashed brains underfoot, eyes that belong to no owner, tongues without land or sky, ears that are like whelks in the beaches of the ghosts, Maria! . . . Maria . . . The embrace. The fingers fondle the loose hair of the *doek.*[1] The hands shake. Can't you speak? . . . Maria . . . Tomorrow, Maposse, we'll go to Shakir's store to exchange the mealie and the chestnuts . . . Maria, speak, Maria . . . We'll take João, yes, we'll take João . . . where's João, Maria? . . . The bloodied hands run through the body, they are hindered by the eyes out of their sockets, they glide through the endless scratches, skirt past the scattered bruises, detain themselves in the lacerated thighs; the eyes shudder, the head of the woman, like a *maçala*[2] of prehistoric size, falls, grazing the naked trunk. You are naked . . . They touched you . . . The tears slide down the sorrowful face, Maria . . . It's night, a dog barks, the cattle in the pen are uneasy, the sacred tree frees some of its irksome leaves, the hands reach closer, grope, the water's pale strip shudders, the bodies cling together, the man rows, the body moves forward, retreats and advances; the ship sways, the sides shake, the prow rises with the force of a wave, liturgical dances conjure the evil-bearing spirits of the sea, the waves quieten, the prow is lowered in the waddling of exorcists in ecstasy, the man rows, the body moves forward, retreats; the moon laughs, the man's teeth look like fireflies turned to stone in the darkness of the night, the sweat runs, it is mixed with the salty waters that persist in running through the anchorage which receives them with the prolonged sighs of a quelled unease, aaah . . . You are mine . . . They touched you . . . The *capulana*³ covers the body. The eyelids hide the eyes. The face takes on the form of those dead whose earthly sorrow had been too great. My son? Is he alive? He looks around again. The same silence. The same sound. The same voice. The same absence. João! Silence. The sounds of the footsteps reverberate. The village is in mourning. The night darkness grows. The sounds of the steps are like thunder. The eyes look searchingly. The body shudders. He's standing at the street corner of a wrecked road clogged up with corpses. He stops. The eyes run through the corpses, both the ones he knew and the unrecognisable. The street is a butchery that trades in human flesh. Arms that belong to no one; legs hanging from imaginary rings; hearts in mounds of sand; livers on display like jellyfish on the remains of a shipwreck; penises suspended from poles, proclaiming the end of creation; hands rising out of swamps of blood; faces, immobile, anguished, terrified, faces that have no life. The man moves away. He runs. Flees. Shouts. Stumbles. Falls. Rolls on the ground. Faints. João! . . .

'They have killed us.'

He wiped the tears.

I have to find him, he said to himself as he set out to return to the village whose outline he couldn't make out for it was covered by a thick cloud. What would it be? . . . Swarms of flies hovered above the destroyed village. Shafts of moonlight cut spaces in the cloud of flies. He made a pathway with the help of his hands, just as he had done a while ago with the twigs and the leaves and the boughs of the forest of the gods which he had penetrated with the purpose of presenting the gods with the gifts he had promised to offer on behalf of Maria, barren woman, as the village rumour was wont to go, from door to door, from cattle pen to cattle pen, kitchen to kitchen, yard to yard, right up to the nearby river where the women with many-shaped

jugs harangued over Maria who would not bear a child, for as a
young girl she had dared to slander the ancestral spirits of Feniasse,
the old blind woman, who had sworn with mythological certainty
that the woman whose voice uttered such blasphemies would not
conceive a child, a version of the story denied by others who had
known Maria since childhood and who affirmed with equal certainty
that she had been born a virgin and married a virgin, and she herself
had never even vilified the fly that had dared to place itself on the
wooden bowl containing the vegetables of her malnourished meal, a
variant of the story accepted by many others who vouched for the
fact that the spirits and the blind were often mistaken, and in this
hurly-burly the women, jugs on their heads, drew closer to the
village, casting looks of contempt and of pity and of sadness which
Maposse, basket-weaver of note, accepted with a feigned pride, but
which drove him to tears during the nights when he prayed to the
good-bearing spirits of his clan, spirits who had come to his help, two
months before, during a night without moon when she had proudly
proclaimed that the moon did not exist, a statement which made him
redouble his, country-wise, gestures of affection right up to the
afternoon when she, to the dismay and rejoicing of many, delivered
the liberating howl to the sky of straw and the beams of the hut
which shuddered like the forest did on that day of offerings to the
spirits whom the twigs and the leaves and the boughs protected with
the same tenacity of Shaka's guards and with the certainty that the
night is not the most appropriate time for oblations, for the spirits,
like those who dwell on the earth, divest themselves of the clinical
solemnity of protocol and hand themselves over to the depravity that
the ethics of both living and dead relegate to the wild night, but I,
Maposse by birth, shall enter into your kingdom in the fullness of
night and I shall be offering you the oblation that I had promised,
and it was with this certainty that he routed the army of twigs and
boughs and leaves, and walked inside the circle of both ancient and
more recent spirits who, lost in some indescribable amorous languor
as sepulchral music played on, did not notice him until the moment
of pause and surprise, for all, caught in the misdoing, felt and saw
the incredulous stare of Maposse to whom it had never occurred that
the spirits would so readily embrace the orgies that in life they
condemned and whose condemnation he adhered to with the
innocence of neophytes frightened with tales of morality which grew

with the wavering flames of the nameless firesides on the fields which rose up, like his, in front of the big house where his grandfather, the same one that looked at him with the dehydrated countenance of someone who had been embalmed by someone who suffered from chronic diarrhoea, went out in search of him, always catching him in the act, the cause of much joy to him, for the curses only ended when they sat around the fireside where they were seasoned with the stories of ogres which terrorized him on sleepless nights, And today, the same grandfather was saying, you have stumbled on a serious misdeed, and if death does not embrace you here and now it is because your son awaits you, Don't open your mouth, my filthy dog, what you see here is not the shame of the earth, but the liturgical dances of purification beyond the tomb which your people, filthy, will never be able to understand, And on the day that you dare recount what you have seen your tongue will fall out of your mouth, Go, run to the pallet of your son who will grow like the others and will die after a long old age, He disappeared from sight and didn't hear any more because he found himself holding his child in his trembling arms in the hut of his life, surrounded by friends who greeted him and whom he thanked, not them but the spirits, who protected the boy until the age when he could run with the cattle through the savannah and the open treeless plains where they roasted rats in the flames of the night, eating them with his father who dribbled with satisfaction, not only for the tasty flesh but also for the mugs of *xicadju*, name given in these parts to the juice of the cashew, prepared by the woman who was anxious to hear from her husband, already half drunk, stories from the distant lands of the Ronga where he had tried his luck on the tarred roads of dawn, always carrying the buckets of shit of his survival. No, it shan't be these mad dogs who'll be taking life away from my son . . . .

'João!'

The flies, moving around with blatant aerobatics, shared the remnants of the echo out amongst themselves.

He looked around. Streams of distant moonlight collapsed on the ground without even the din of agony. From space to space, like post-diluvial craters, emerged wells of light. The walls, broken down, thrown open, looked like zimbabwes of lost times smiling with nostalgia before the shafts of moonlight that made the incurable sores waste away, in the doors of the tomb, the ransacked rooms, the halls of the last supper and the verandahs of the Pompeii of modern times. The toilets, without embarrassment, threw disjointed mouths at the stalactites of the moon, calling out to clients with the most ridiculous faces in the world.

'João!'

Silence. Humming sounds. The void.

He looks at the sky of flies. He was inside the circle. Death ran through that circle. Blood grew slack within the circle. The spirits ran through the circle. The corpses became rotten within the circle. The flies danced on the circle. They laughed in the circle. Ate in the circle. Lived in the circle.

'João!'

A shout that would not resound. An anguished look. Dead gestures. I am dead. I am a ghost. I am among the spirits.

I am dead! he shouted. He didn't hear his own shout. He could not feel the ownerless bowels under his feet, or the severed hands, the gangrenous heads, the broken backs, the eyes burst open, the decomposing flesh, the flies wallowing in the liquid of the dead, the blood in clots, the colourless faeces, the lakes of piss, the sea of vomit, the rivers of blood. I couldn't feel anything. I walked like a ghost. He walked. Walked.

'Father!'

A voice.

He halted.

He turned his body.

'Who is it?'

A dying voice.

'It's me.'

'Who?'

'Your son.'

'You are dead.'

'I am alive.'

'You don't exist.'

Silence. A young body walked out of the reed latrine.

'I'm your son João.'

Maposse's hands felt the young body; the fingers ran through the face and the neck, stopping at the frail shoulders. They looked at each other.

'You don't exist, João.'

'I am alive.'

'No one is alive. We're dead. We are anguished spirits in search of a decent tomb. It's the others who're still alive, João.'

'What others?'

Maposse did not reply. He unloosened his hands from the shoulders, looked at the boy and walked away from the area, hounded by the insatiable flies.

translated by Luís Rafael

1 A scarf wrapped round the head.
2 A fruit.
3 A colourful cloth worn as a sarong-style garment.

BALEKA KGOSITSILE
Where is Home

Tell me
where is home
Is it the hotel room
which hosts
this grand occasion
which presides
over this honour
which delivers to me
the first sleep
inside my country
after 5148 nights
away from home
down the thin road
of personal history
roaming
in search of home

Tell me
where is home
Is it the cluster
of mud structures
which surround
my father's ageing body
and lonely heart
is it the thorny path
to the family graveyard
could it be the shade
of the tall trees
whispering above
my mother's grave

or the sacred space
which permanently holds
her body away
from my hungry eye

Is home the house
in Lusaka or
my children in it
is it the flat
I sneak in and out of
unnoticed
where is it
is it the elusive roof
turning me fast into
an olympic candidate
as apartheid grins
at me daily
its green teeth
mocking my enquiries
systematically turning
my coming home
to a jump
into a bottomless pit

Listen
is it the corner
on Leopold street
packed with women
children and belongings
night after winter
night while fate
sits huddled
in a warm corner
watching . . .
biding its time

eyes glued
on the boxing ring
to our surprise
left to words
thin-legged words
without gloves
flying round the ring
not even a referee in sight
is this it

Where is home
tell me
Is it childhood
memories that weathered
exile storms
is it the square
shoulder that supports
my wet face
where is it
I search the eyes
of my comrades
while we *toyi-toyi*[1]
on the back
of the truck
which is breaking all
speed limits
heading irreversibly
for Mhlanga rocks
where . . . where is it

What shall I tell
my children's children
Their birth was postponed
when history possessed by
an unspeakable zeal

poured thirty years
of golden honey
into the dough
of the home cake
where is it
please answer me
is it in the kneading
basin or the oven
where is it
my womb asks persistently
while faithfully clutching
at the bouquet
of feather dreams

If home is South Africa
a country in the
continent of Africa
if it is the world
sprawling across planet earth
let it have
a plate of food for all
let it fill
winter mornings with
the sunshine of human
goodwill pouring from hearts
of clothed women
men and children
free from homelessness
free from fear
free from jealousy
free from humiliation

Let it come
with torrents of rain
to wash away
bloodstains tears and gall

141

of yesterday
let this moment
turn into home
the bull's eye of the
prisoner's focus
as minute after ticking
minute defines and moulds
dedication and discipline

Home
the heart of hope
for the scrawny youngster
'I don't know where home is
violence or forced removals
moved my village'
he says and continues
to arm hundreds
with the art
of fighting a disciplined war
his love of home
an elaborate song
known best by his heart
and the sands of Angola

Let home feed music
into the silence
surrounding the memory
of the ex-prisoner
let home be
an unfolding dawn
ushering in the new day
where my daughter
will be seen and
judged as a person
let it bring us eyes

142

that will see
voices that will sing
the beautiful things
around us
let it be
the symphony that
will massage
the tension lines
from the weary heart
of our people
that will water
the seed of a future
determined to be born
that the children
of this country
be midwife and parent
to HOME

1 *Toyi-toyi*: militant dance.

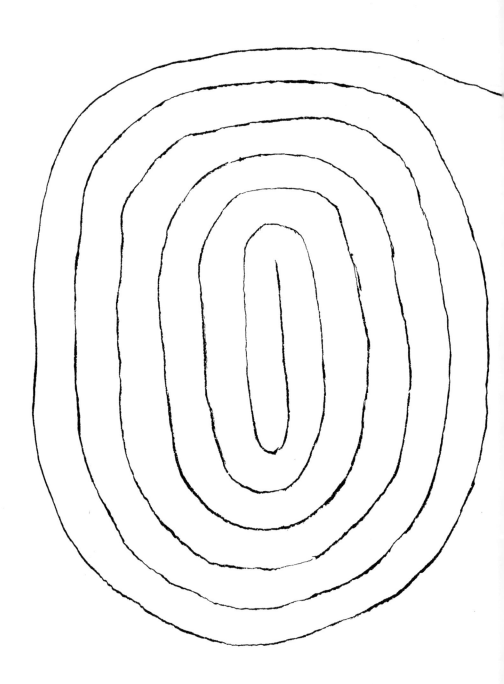

LIZ GUNNER
The Two of Us

I can't remember exactly when I put Mother Africa out in the garden but I know I did so with a twinge of guilt. She came from Sierra Leone and was bent at the knees and had a sharp belly and unapologetic pendulous breasts. I think when she first went outside she still had arms, bent at the elbow, angular, but the tell-tale holes were there – the beetles were eating away at her inside. I had to put her out or they would burrow into the woodwork, into the sturdy mahogany table, gnaw into everything, uncontrollable. So I put her in the back garden and she stood lurchingly with her bent knees – a bit like Lear braving the elements, I suppose.

She stood in the grass and the children rushed past on their way to play out in the sportsfield beyond the back alley. They didn't ask who she was and I didn't tell them. They did know about Africa though – photographs, me, their South African Mum, visitors with strange accents who picked them up when they were little and made them laugh a lot.

The weather got worse and the beetles must have been eating away – she fell over. What could I do with her? I couldn't bury her, I couldn't forget her, I couldn't use her for firewood. So I put her in the shed with its dusty glass panels, its mystery, its wonderful clutter and awayness – and there was famine in Ethiopia, famine in Somalia and really the mothers of Africa were starving and fighting for life. And in Eritrea and in the South the young lionesses were fighting alongside the men – at least I think so, and it had something to do with her, but I'm not sure what.

Well, the seasons passed. The children grew and fewer visitors with rich accents and deep laughs came. The children's guinea-pigs died of pneumonia or old age and the rebel bluebells in the garden came up year after year, next to the genteel phlox with the lingering sweet scent, and the delicate bleeding heart with its tiny red hearts hung on graceful and drooping stems. And of all of these, the bluebells would never go away because long before there was a house here – and that was a hundred years or so – there had been an orchard, and before that fields, and they had always been there. No amount of poking with a trowel or digging deep with a garden fork and bringing up the sticky, opaque bulbs, could expel them. I knew, inside me, that I would die and they would still be there, but her, my Mother Africa with her broken arms and leg, silent and stubborn and prone in the shed of secrets and children's games. What would become of her? And of me?

The Africa thing had never been easy. You said, 'Yiss', you appeared at people's houses without phoning first, you tried to look at the terrible South from a distance, understand it from the cold safety of six thousand miles. You sat like a stone in green English fields because in your head you lived with rocks of wild unspeakable shapes and vast distances that would eat England like a crumb. But I had gone through that; the rocks had sunk back, the distances just sang sometimes in my bones, and only once, with a shock slap, Khambula Mountain struck my face – translating itself from a hill in the Peak District, without the ghosts of the Zulu and British dead. I really had almost forgotten.

And then the new faces came. I was unprepared, and I didn't know where you were. Perhaps stubbornly rotting but refusing to die in the dark garden shed with the forgotten guinea-pigs. This time there was no landscape. People.

'You can tell where Orlando ends. There's no sign, not even barbed wire. But Soweto people just know. When we were going to school we just knew – this is where it begins.'

'Children are innocent,' I said.

'Children are *not* innocent,' the man with unflinching eyes flung back at me. 'They have seen a woman's eyes pop from her head as the necklace flames crackled. *You* are the innocent one.' His eyes mocked me.

And you laughed and wept for me with your crooked knees and I think you wept for the children as well.

I should have known there was no escaping.

Sobantu with the lazy white homes of Scottsville over its shoulder and the veld inbetween. Over the youth-club piano blues Henry grins, 'People are going. People are simply melting away. You go for them and hei! *Abekho!* They've gone. You don't ask where. But we all know!'

I go home, shortcutting the veld way on my moped and the country howls in the State of Emergency. In Scottsville the night streets are very, very quiet, night lights, broad easy streets of 'Maritzburg city, but no people. We are all afraid. Saracens group like vultures in the townships. Some of us listen to Makeba. Like a diviner she sings to us in our quiet student rooms and we cling to her voice.

The quiet woman with the smooth face and pink uniform tells me from the kitchen, 'I have heard from Chief Luthuli. I have had a letter, he says we are to strike. The whole nation will strike and we will bring *iHulumeni*[1] to its knees. MaHadebe you were very brave, and the old chief.

Courage like the incoming tide lapping around my feet.

'It's hard,' he says. 'You come here and you know you must bury your accent, you must blend in. You mustn't talk about Benoni, not in Cambridge, not in Bournemouth, not anywhere. You can't say, "*Man but it's a helluva schlep!*" You just iron it all out. *Lekker* must go. *Voetsak, naartjies, takkies* – put them all in a carton outside the back door. Then you sit in the underground and hear South Africans and you rush up and say, "Hey! I'm from South Africa!" And they say, "And so?" Man! you feel such a fool!'

So you play Ladysmith Black Mambazo and then Stravinsky and talk about Julian Barnes – but read Coetzee, Anthony Sher as well, keep Serote on the shelf in your room. And you hope that the voices in your head will all talk nicely to each other and it'll be awright. Boy, I feel for you, don't hide it, let it all come bubbling up, it's your lifestream.

We pulled down the shed. It came down quite easily. It had been sloping on one side for a long time, rotting at the base although some of the timbers were still beautifully strong. We took everything out. In the shed it had all been our other selves, safe, out of time, out of the regularity of meals, of those who lived by the rule of cars and dustbin collections and getting up and sleeping and living in Thatcher's Britain, Callaghan's paradise and before that, in the state governed by the man with the pointed nose and stubby fingers who loved music and the sea.

We destroyed our darkness — the shed pieces were put out on other people's tips or went out to the dustmen. We stared at bare and neat cement and a tidy brick wall. But she came inside, painfully full of holes and her face rotting too now. I hid her in a cupboard and went away searching for Africa. I went a long way, far from the solid house and the bluebells, but when I came back like a ghost, a memory, I opened the cupboard in the kitchen and she was there, lying on her side, and I was so happy.

1 *iHulumeni*: the government

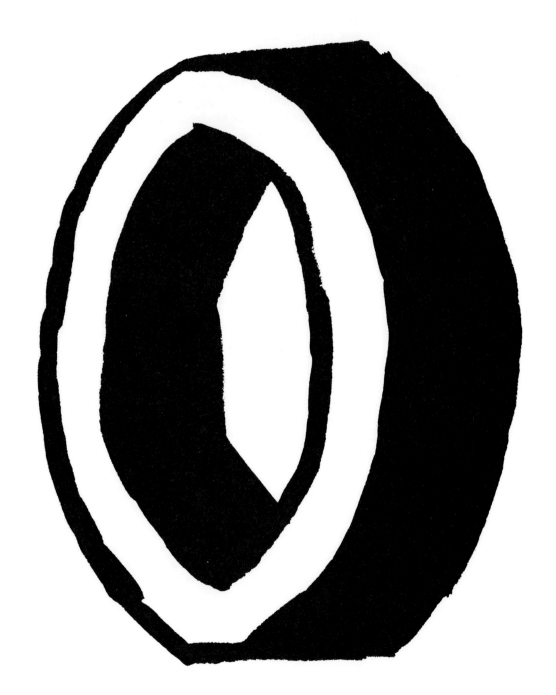

LIZ GUNNER
The Mandela Days

So we took him at dead of night and wrapped him in the skin of the beast we had slaughtered for him. We left our place, quietly, so that the dogs of our neighbours wouldn't bark, and we went a distance with him, putting the body in the open truck and driving with no headlights to the forest, the gumtrees at Stamford, not so far from the sea where the old king had crossed the water into exile after the war with the English.

Sipho had brought a spade. We didn't want to throw him into the forest like a dog. He was our son, our kinsman, my child. So we took spades and dug him a grave, not deep because it would attract suspicion even in this time of killing and dying, and it would take time.

We gave him a shallow grave, our Njomane, our young son who had followed the wrong path and gone with the enemy. Brave, like the old Njomane —

> You who went away for years
> But in the fourth year we saw you again!

Our young one, following where we told him not to go.

The skin of the beast was stiff, like his young body and they fitted awkwardly into the hole, deep enough for dogs not to sniff and for the stench of decay to be lost. So we threw earth over him and his wrong ways, asking in our hearts, *How could you follow a stranger from another nation,*

go with people who burnt and killed and looted and turned children against their elders and make them dance mad dances learnt in the countries to the north?

Follow a stranger who had spent long years in jail far away in the south, a man who knew nothing of our lives here, our ways.

*Singing their mad songs which made you wild with reckless joy —
Tambo, Mandela, Sisulu, Slovo we have never seen them.*

Our son, why did you do this?

But this is not the end of it. People will know that we lost a son.

Women will tell his story and the fearfulness of it. That out of shame or scorn or anger, or was it fear they took his body and threw it to the dogs far away from the homestead, far from the ancestors, and they will never sing his song with the others. They will talk about us in quiet huts at funerals when the women sit alone guarding the body of the mourned one and what we have done will be a sign of the country dying.

Why did he ask so many questions?

Baba, who is Mandela? Why do we sit with so little and the long cars speed up and down the black road? What is the history of our part, before the sugar came? before the whites came?

Better to have had him dull and quiet but still with the smile and the laughter.

Baba, is it true that the old people called it Ematafeni, because it was like a great green plain scattered with cattle and homesteads stretching out as far as the eye could see, when you came down from the hills to the north, from Hlabisa? And they say it was rich with people and cattle and it was Dube territory, and Mjadu territory. Father tell me, is this true? And ourselves, the Mhlongos, the People of the Sun we have been here for long years? Isn't it so?

And you who rush along the black tarred road with the speed of meteors and see only the tattered huts and thin cattle and the limping men, know that you see nothing.

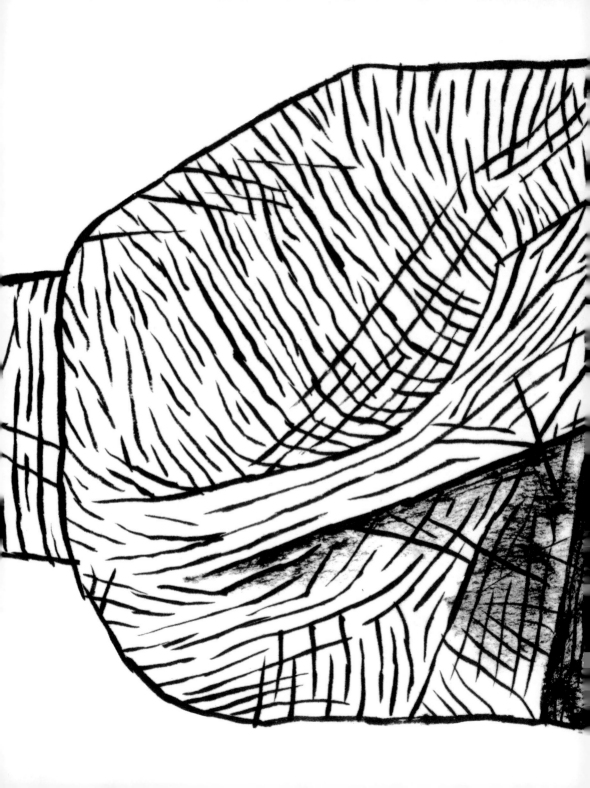

HENRY INDANGASI
The Smoke

'As I was saying, before we were interrupted by that waiter, there are moments when you wish you could live your life again, or retrace your steps, to find out exactly where you branched off in the wrong direction. My ambition was to live a useful life, become a writer, or even a *professor* like you,' he said, emphasising the word 'professor' with what sounded to me like a tinge of irony. We were drinking beer in Stand Bar at Chavakali Market.

'I'll ignore the sarcasm in your tone,' I told him and smiled.

'No, no. You misunderstand me. I have a lot of respect for you and your colleagues in the academic profession,' he protested.

'The point is, I wanted to be happy. But as you know, my undergraduate performance was terminally deplorable. And then my marriage – well, you came to my wedding, I remember – yes, that marriage was an unmitigated disaster.'

'Oh! I'm sorry to hear that. What happened?'

'I can see we haven't been in touch for a long time . . . Having come from a family with *mbesha*[1], as our Kikuyu friends say, she started to despise me. I could have lived with it if it had remained verbal, but then early one morning, coming back home from Eregi Teachers' College, I found her with her lover in the bedroom . . . Well, we are now divorced.'

'This might sound like the wisdom of hindsight, but I have never stopped wondering how you got emotionally entangled in the first place. Musimbi struck me as incurably vain . . . But I'm sure she has her own side of the story.'

'Well, I started by telling you about retracing my steps. My experience with Musimbi gave prominence to a romantic encounter I had many years ago, but which I kept locked up in my system. I don't know whether you want to hear it. It's such a pity, but the thing is, the kind of suffering I have undergone makes you so self-centred you always want other people to listen to you. Forgive me if it looks like that.'

'Don't philosophise,' I said, smiling. 'Tell me the story.'

'Waiter,' he called. 'Bring us some more Exports.'

I was the duty master that week at Ngusimu High School during the April vacation when she came. I had not expected any of the delegates to the Friends' Yearly Meeting to arrive that evening. According to the instructions I received from Mr Igonga, the headmaster, they were supposed to come the following day.

She was wearing a pink headkerchief, pink stockings, a white nylon dress and white high-heeled shoes. Her face was yellowish-brown, and she had *isang'ali*, a gap in her front teeth, which had a brown coloration, the typical effect of excess fluoride in some of our Kenyan waters. She wore no lipstick on her thick, fleshy, sensuous lips; and there was a marked contrast in her eyes between the pupils which were very dark and the eyeballs which were very white. And I thought there was a preoccupied, faraway look in those eyes, which she would half-close whenever she talked.

'Good afternoon, Madam,' I said, shaking her slim, rather delicate hand.

'Good afternoon, Sir,' she answered.

'We didn't expect you this early, but you are most welcome.'

'Well, I knew I would arrive a day early, but you see, I have come all the way from Elburgon. It's my first time to come to Kakamega District, so I had to give myself time to look for this place.'

'Never mind. We'll do something. It's just that I can't open a whole dormitory for you . . . But we should have started at the beginning by introducing ourselves. My name is John Akivambo, and I'm the master-on-duty this week.'

'I'm Peninnah Wangui, a typist at a *harambee* school in Elburgon.'

'It's fascinating. You're the first Kikuyu Quaker I've met.'

'I figured you'd say something like that. We are not many. I was in fact introduced to Quakerism by some Luhya friends who have settled in Elburgon. So here I am,' she said, the last sentence sounding as if it contained a note of defiance. But she quickly checked herself, and blushed.

I had just done my A-levels at Ngasimuka High, another Quaker school in this province, and was working as an untrained teacher while I waited to go to the University of Nairobi. For me, it was a transitional stage, when you imagine you are about to hop from poverty to wealth, and when the world promises money, happiness and love. So, in fact, I thought her words were a challenge, the nature of which I could not quite define.

'I don't know how to put it, but I'm all alone in my house. There is plenty of room, and you're welcome to stay with me tonight,' I told her.

We were standing outside the staffroom which was locked because, as I said, my colleagues were on vacation. When I said this, she shrugged her shoulders and looked sideways.

'That's kind of you. I do appreciate the offer,' she said, looking at her shoes. But her eyes seemed to say I have no choice in the matter.

I got hold of her suitcase, and together we walked to my house.

'Welcome,' I said, as I opened the door for her. 'This is where I live.'

'H'm, you have a big house.'

'You see, the Teachers' Service Commission gives me a beggarly salary, but fools me with a big house.'

She laughed and said, 'Well, what would a typist in a *harambee* school say to that? My house and my salary are both beggarly, to use your word.'

Realising that I should have counted my blessings and named them one by one, I quickly changed the topic.

'I'll fix *ugali*[2] for supper, although I know you're used to *irio*.'[3]

'Me, I can eat anything that is eaten by other human beings. In fact I eat a lot of *ugali* with my Luhya friends in Elburgon; I've even eaten it with *mrenda*.'[4]

After supper, I told Peninnah that I had two bedrooms, and that she could either sleep in the spare one, or share the main one with me. She smiled and shook her head, saying, 'I know what you'll think, but I'll sleep in the spare bedroom.'

Yes, I figured you would laugh . . . One would say that as a circumcised red-blooded Luhya young man, I should not have taken no for an answer, and that I should have begged and insisted. But I wanted to see myself as high-minded and morally sensitive. Besides, my A-level literary background had predisposed me to the feminist idea.

So, I smiled back, stood up, walked her to the spare bedroom, made the bed for her and good night.

If I told you I went to the bed and slept immediately, I would be lying. The image of this strange, beautiful woman kept hovering around me. I would close my eyes and still see her. I don't quite remember, but I must have dozed off at three or so in the morning.

It was with a strange ticklish feeling that I woke up around seven. My first desire was to go and check in her bedroom, perhaps to be sure that fate had not played a practical joke on me; but I decided instead to fix breakfast so that when I went there it would be to invite her to come and eat.

On seeing me open her bedroom door, she turned her head and tried to cover her face with the bedsheet; but suddenly she changed her mind and smiled the same ironic smile I had noticed the previous day.

'Good morning,' I said.

'Good morning, John,' she replied.

'Did you enjoy your sleep?'

'Yes, I did . . . in this strange land. How about you?' she asked with a chuckle.

'I did, but for some time before I slept I thought about you.'

'Was there anything to think about? Did I upset you?' she asked with calculated irony.

'Well, not really. Just the romantic setting of our encounter. Our meeting is more interesting than any I have read about in fiction.'

I was in an effusive mood, but I wasn't sure she got my message. After a few seconds, she said, 'Fortunately, you won't have to think again. At least not with me on the other side of your bedroom wall . . . You will open the dormitories as soon as the other delegates arrive, won't you?'

'Of course I will . . . I came to announce that breakfast is ready.'

'You should have asked me to help. I'm not used to men cooking for me. But give me ten minutes. I need to take a quick shower.'

I didn't have much of an appetite, but for her part she seemed to be enjoying my bachelor breakfast, scrambled eggs, bread and tea.

'You are a good cook,' she remarked.

'I've never thought of it that way, but I feel flattered.'

'What's on your mind?' she asked after a few minutes of silence.

'Nothing really. I was just wondering, won't you come back for supper? As you know, I'm not attending your meetings. My job is to ensure there is no disturbance.'

'I'll try to. But why won't you attend our meetings?'

'I wasn't invited. Besides, I happen not to be a believer.'

'H'm, what a pity. Not a believer?'

'Don't let the confession bother you.'

'I think it will. I have interacted with Muslims and Christians of other denominations, but this is the very first time I've met a non-believer. Are you what people call a devil-worshipper, or what?'

'No, no. I believe in something, though not a supreme being.'

'What's that something?'

'Humanism, the general well-being of humanity.'

'I don't understand. But isn't that what Christianity is all about?'

'Perhaps, but I don't have to go to church to believe in the welfare of human beings. Besides, Christianity is full of dogmas, there is a lot of thou shalt not, about which you can't argue.'

'Not Quakerism though. We believe in that of God in every man. But your views are puzzling, and I guess you'll tell me more about them when I come back,' she said, and after a few seconds, 'if I do, that is.'

'You really must for supper here. Then I'll tell you how I parted company with the Quakers, even though they educated me.'

After she left for her meeting, I wandered aimlessly on the school compound. We had some incorrigible thieves among our school cooks; and in fact on an earlier occasion I had caught one of them carrying sugar in his gumboots. But on this day, I didn't feel like supervising them. The Quakers were singing and praying, but these activities did not register in my mind.

Try as I would, I could not get over this stranger. It's true: having abandoned religion, I embraced the notion of scientific progress. I believed in the infinite perfectibility of men and women. Religious dogma inhibited our rational thinking which was essential if we were to develop to a higher moral level.

But just now, I was thinking of some omnipotent force called fate, which had brought this attractive lady into my lonely life in this rural secondary school.

Peninnah came back around four, just after her fellow delegates had gone for tea.

'I have come early. They are meeting again in the evening, but I don't know whether I want to go back,' she said, half-closing her eyes.

'Forget about it then. Just stay here with me. They also serve the Lord, who sit and wait, said an English poet.'

'Don't say that. Coming all the way from Elburgon, just to stay with a stranger in Luhyaland, and more so a non-believer?' she asked and added, 'I came here in search of God, not a lover.' But I could sense she wanted to stay.

The delegates were there for three days, but she did not witness much of what took place. She would often excuse herself and come over to my house. And strange as it may sound, we both lost interest in the intellectual debate about believers and non-believers. The one thing we cared about was to be together and to listen to what our hearts were telling us.

We were sitting in the living room on the third day when we heard a loud hissing sound coming from the kitchen. I jumped up and ran to rescue the cabbage I had left on the electric cooker, groped through the thick smoke and switched it off.

Peninnah had rushed after me, and as we stood there, breathing with difficulty and looking at the black, sooty mess on the *sufuria*, she leaned on me and kissed me with a passion I have not forgotten to this day.

'Let's go back to the living room,' she said. 'We'll be choked to death. How could you be so forgetful?' she said, laughing.

'Well . . .' I fumbled.

'We'll count our losses. I'm not really hungry, but we can go to a kiosk for a snack.'

'Okay, let's go,' I said, thinking of my last two pounds.

She returned very early the following morning, when the other delegates were preparing to leave.

'Here I am again. I'm supposed to leave for Elburgon, but my heart tells me to stay. I could live with you for ever.'

But romance costs money. I longed to say *Yes*, stay and be my wife. Unfortunately, I was broke in the most meaningful sense of the word. The month was twenty-something, and the Teachers' Service Commission used to pay us, as indeed they still do, at the beginning of the following month. Besides, having spent my meagre salary paying school fees for my brothers and sisters, I was simply waiting for the next payment with which I would prepare to go to university.

I took Peninnah to the Siganga bus stop and bade her goodbye. Tears were rolling from her eyes as she got on to the bus that was travelling to Nakuru. Up above, dark ominous clouds had formed, and it looked as if we would have another of those heavy rains that are typical of our Kakamega weather. As the bus moved away, I felt something heavy in my throat. I quickly walked back to my vacant house, lay on my bed and cursed my fate profusely.

'Did you see her again?' I asked after a long pause, having listened keenly to his story.

'No, I never did. We wrote to each other for a while after I had joined the University of Nairobi, and she kept reminding me of her offer to marry me . . . No, I missed the opportunity. I had no money to marry, and my parents were poor . . . Peninnah, I learnt later, married another man.

'But the memory of her kiss in my smoky kitchen has refused to die. I have travelled to several corners of our great republic, dimly hoping to see her one more time, but in vain.'

'And your belief in humanism? You know, that interests me as an academician,' I said, trying to relieve the pain of his story.

'Well, we'll talk about that another time . . .'

We finished our drinks and left for our different *nyalgungas*, our rural homes.

1 Money,
2 A stiff porridge.
3 A dish of mashed beans, maize and potatoes.
4 A green leafy vegetable.

FRANK MEINTJIES
Rhythms of Passage 1

from byways to skyways through fourways
keyholed through subways oneways slipways
and rights of way

spiderwebbing's time to shine
what gleams at am is smogged over by pm
rooftops, pylons, factories, transmitters
hang from invisible hands

resting on one leg at a time

in fetters, to courthouse or stokkies
on the meat-tray of an ambulance
one piston beat behind conveyor belt
surface or underground
from state of tension to spate of roadblocks
spanning health conditions
from alertness to drowsing out
suspended from praisehymns
and pounding of a *toyi-toyi*
reflected in a waterdrop eye

intersecting with dispatch
with all that's boxed and packed
for the long haul
from hand to mouth
over the spine of a minedump
hitting the city beat
along trimmed-edges of gardens
the taken-for-granted undercoating
to the happy Kodak snap

checking my way 'round everything

CORNELIA SMITH
The White Dove

'You have contracted an opportunistic infection in your lungs, Mr Pailman,' the doctor said, 'I'm afraid you will have to be admitted to hospital for treatment.'

Robin Pailman bowed his head, cradling it in his thin, brown hands.

'I must warn you about the severity of the situation,' the doctor continued. He frowned at Robin: 'Where were you for the past three months, Mr Pailman? Why did you stop coming for counselling and treatment?'

Robin was silent. Pastor Abe had said that he would not need medical treatment, that he should leave everything to the Lord. After Robin had publicly repented for his great sin, and promised to lead a reformed life, Pastor Abe had laid his hands on him to heal him. After that Robin prayed every day to thank the Lord for healing him and went to church on Sundays and sometimes on Wednesdays too; he donated a third of his salary to the church, but the coughing and diarrhoea did not stop. Now he became short of breath at the slightest exertion, felt listless and very tired. The sores in his mouth made it difficult to eat and he was so thin that his bones and enlarged glands protruded under his loose, sallow skin.

'You people should all be locked up away from society,' the doctor said suddenly. Like Robin he was one of those people who, in spite of evidence to the contrary, firmly believed that AIDS was a homosexual disease.

'You think you can flout all the rules of God and society and escape divine punishment . . .' He stopped, struggling to regain his professional amiability.

Robin raised his head and looked at the doctor. Tears filled his eyes.

The doctor was angry and embarrassed at losing control over his feelings. He frowned, concentrating on a spot above Robin's head. Robin pulled himself together, scrubbing at his tears angrily. Slowly he rose from the chair and stumbled towards the door. A short man, delicately built, he looked almost like a child now. Behind him the doctor was shouting something about the grave prognosis if he should continue in this foolhardy way. But was life worth living like this? Robin closed the door of the way consulting room carefully.

Outside he leaned against the wall to catch his breath, and walking thus, resting every few steps, he reached the waiting room where his friend, Alex, was waiting. Alex jumped up to assist him. Slowly they made their way to the car. Alex helped him in, adjusting the seat to a semi-upright position, putting a small pillow under his head, covering him with a crocheted bedspread.

Robin kept remembering the picture that used to hang above his bed when he was a child. It was of Jesus in flowing robes, holding his hands out to a white dove flying above his head. He had not been healed by him after all, Robin thought. The tears returned and he lost control. Dry, grunting sobs seemed to be wrenched from his soul. Alex made soothing noises, holding him until he was quiet. By then he felt totally drained.

'Forgive me, Alex,' he whispered later that evening when it was time for Alex to go. Alex ran his young, strong hand through his blond hair and nodded. He kissed Robin before saying goodbye. But Robin was referring to more than his earlier breakdown; he was also apologising because he had asked Alex to leave the semi-detached house in Mayfair that they had shared for two years.

Robin could not fall asleep. His mind raced in circles: from the day he was told of his illness to his denial, pretending that it had never happened. He thought with bitterness about the loss of his career as a teacher when his illness became known. The loss of the few friends he had made, living in a grey area as he did, only filled him with contempt; but underneath the contempt there was the pain of rejection. His anger that this should be happening to him surfaced again. And every time his thoughts returned to his religious conversion and the healing ceremony, he would ask: What went wrong? Why wasn't I saved? Was my faith not strong enough, as they said? Underscoring all these thoughts was his fear: What will happen to me now? At this point it seemed an iron vice gripped his chest.

He decided to have a soft drink and shuffled to the kitchen. He thought about his mother's half-hearted offer to come and look after him. He had been a disappointment to her although he had tried so hard to please her. He sat down at the table remembering his disastrous marriage.

Seventeen years ago. He had not thought about it for a long time. He wondered about his children: Dick would be about fifteen now, and Sandy nine.

He began wondering about the purpose of his life on earth . . . Did he fulfil this purpose? His children, were they the purpose of his life on earth? Thank God he had children. He was going to die soon. The thought shocked him to a sudden stillness, but he was not shying away from it any more. At the age of 37, relatively young still, he was going to die.

The need to see his children burned inside him and he decided to call his mother. In his room he stood in front of the wardrobe, taking a black notebook from a metal box containing two gold coins, a gun, his will, and some insurance papers. With trembling fingers he found his mother's number and dialled.

It rang for a long time.

'Hello?' a voice said impatiently.

'Hello, Mother . . . it's Robin . . . how are you?' he said timidly.

'Oh . . . Robin,' she said. Then: 'Why are you phoning so late? I was busy watching Santa Barbara.'

He looked at his watch, it was just after eight.

'I am sorry, mother. It's just that . . . it is kind of important. I want to ask you something . . . please . . . I would like to see the children.'

He moistened his dry lips with his tongue.

'Are you sure? Is it wise? Won't they also get . . .?'

'No, there would be no danger to them.' A long silence followed.

'Oh, all right,' she said. 'When would you like to see them?'

'It doesn't really matter . . . any time . . . that is convenient.' His fingers tightened around the receiver. 'How about Sunday?'

'Okay, I will bring them on Sunday morning. Goodbye now.'

He replaced the receiver nervously; he was afraid to meet his children. They were so small when he left; what had his mother told them about him? He got into bed and watched the late news on television. There had been another bank robbery, the State President met Nelson Mandela and everybody was worried about the ozone layer. He thought that these things seemed so remote, as if they were happening on another planet. The only reality was inside him now, his preoccupation with his disease and his fear.

The next morning, Saturday, Alex came by on his way to town. Robin asked him to buy a few things for the children.

'Presents,' he urged, 'and rolls and viennas for hot dogs. Children like hot dogs. And ice cream.' He remembered that they had liked ice cream.

He spent the rest of the day making and rejecting plans for how to approach his children. Then while having a shower he noticed two raised, purple marks on his chest. This was another sign of the disease inside his body. He sat on his bed, opened the metal box to look at the gun.

'No,' he whispered vehemently.

His children were coming. And besides, it would be a terrible sin.

Fleetingly he wondered whether, like Macbeth, he was not also steeped in sin 'so far that, should I wade no more, returning would be as tedious as to go o'er . . .' He wished that he could change himself and wipe away the past, but suddenly he became angry at the society which would not accept him for what he was.

Sunday morning dawned and found him feverishly wrapping the presents for the children. He was dressed in a red shirt and a pair of black pants. He opened the presents again to put in each a bar of chocolate, but then he decided that Dick was too old for that, so he opened it again to remove the chocolate. He felt as if fluttering moths had invaded his stomach. He tidied the already tidy house, flicking the duster at imaginary spots. His mother hated a dirty house, cleanliness was next to godliness, she believed.

At last the familiar old car stopped outside. He could see his neighbour, a conservative white lady, peeping from her section of the house. The car left – his mother was not coming in after all – and the children were standing on the green grass on the pavement. He realised that the boy looked exactly like him when he was that age. He looked at him in horror. When they came nearer he noticed the boy's mincing walk, neat blowdried hair, and the earring in his left ear.

Robin was not aware that he was opening the door. They were inside now and the children were seated in the lounge. He went to his room like a sleepwalker and came back with the presents and the metal box.

Later, when the police came they found him making hot dogs and talking to himself. Over and over he kept saying, 'I had to save him. I had to save him. The spirit of God descended like a white dove and I had to save him.'

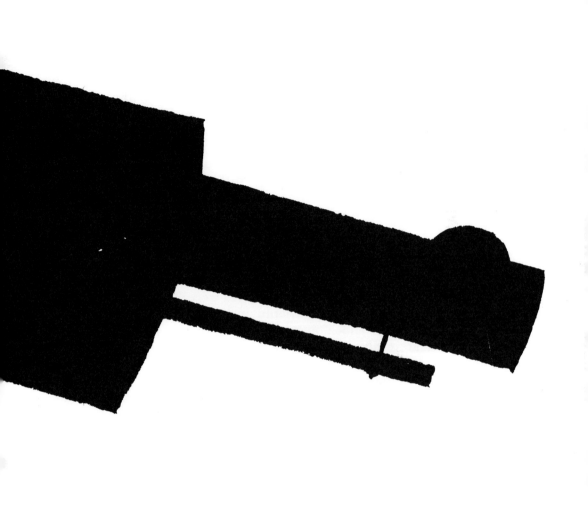

PETER AMUKA
Late

That night I reached home late. In fact very late, because by my wife's standards and rules late began at seven-thirty in the evening, thus making my nine-fifty arrival intolerable.

Not that this particular night's lateness was strange and unprecedented. No. We had been married ten years during which time this woman's strictness and draconian administration regarding time had become so familiar to me they were no different from gulps of water between mouthfuls of a meal.

She had repeatedly warned me that one day I would end up in a lot of trouble. Nights, according to her, were naturally dangerous. There were the omnipresent patrol police wandering all over the city for somebody to arrest or molest. Then there were the gangs who would rob and kill me, or they would kill me for having too little money or nothing at all. Finally there were the roving snakes, spitting a poison that kills the victim instantly. Nevertheless, almost every other night, I ended up repeating the same mistake: coming home late and inspiring the same warning, the same song, so to speak. I had secretly christened her expected yellings 'my arrival-and-welcome-home-anthem'.

And so that night, it should have been the same music, like the proverb of the frog and the bull. Every time the bull went to drink the river water, the frog would croak and croak and jump all over, complaining against the bull's intrusion and hoping that it would be heeded, but the bull never budged until it had had enough. As the saying goes, the croaking of a frog had never made the bull budge. And so here I was waiting to march in pomp to the tune of a familiar song.

I rang the electric bell expecting her to wake up instantly and open the door. No response. I waited and tried again. The same profound silence. That was strange after a decade's consistent obedience, just like a key refusing to open the same door it had been opening for ten years. For the first time it occurred to me that ever since our marriage I had never bothered to carry a spare key.

She was home. She always was. All these years I had found her home much earlier than me, either as a matter of habit or rule or both. With this assurance, I banged the bell again and waited. For five minutes there was still no response. All this time, I kept asking myself whether the frog had overturned the government of the bull. Then, like a godsend, she woke up and switched on the stairway light.

After apparently locating the stairs and estimating the position of the door, she switched off the light. Worse still, she did not spare the security light; it too went off. Whatever was she creating all this darkness for, I wondered. Or was I drunkenly straying into the wrong house? No. That could not be. After all, I was not unconsciously drunk.

I did not hear her footsteps, which were normally very loud be it dark or light. I heard first the slow clicking of the key and the sluggish opening of the door. This must be her, I thought. Come what may and without uttering a word, I plunged into the warm darkness.

My fingers were numb from the cold so I could not switch on the lights. Relying on habit I climbed upstairs toward the bedroom.

As I started fumbling with the bedroom door, I heard loud but leisurely footsteps approaching. Although slow, it was the music of her walk. At once, I knew it was her and seriously wished she could walk even slower just to play a little longer the singing walk that first drew my attention to her and led to the courting and the consequent marriage. That warming music. You saw and heard it with the softest of her movements. Once it started it was a consistent and insistent tune, even if she was immobile. Seated or asleep, you could still hear and see it in the rippling curves of her body. No dress could suppress them. The beat was getting closer and harder, warmer. That music was mounting. My numbness was disappearing with the crescendo of this singing walk.

Then a hard blow landed on my chin, knocking the notes from my ears with a burning effect that seemed to singe my beard. Before the heat had subsided, I sensed another blow coming in the darkness and luckily dodged it as I reached for the light. She was on the corridor floor. Her elbow had missed me and hit the iron doorjamb very hard. She had fallen with a thud and there she was writhing with intense pain and announcing it all in prolonged ear-tearing shrieks; eyes closed as she always did in a temper. When I finally touched her forehead, she kept quiet and seemed to cringe in apparent expectation of a husbandly punitive slap, which contrary to the traditions of society I did not administer. Lifting herself up in stunned surprise, she switched off the light before unlocking the bedroom. She went in, leaving me standing, tongue-tied and wondering why she did not want the light on.

I switched the corridor light on again and stood in the doorway, thinking that she had probably invited a lover to the house and was trying to hide him in the darkness to facilitate his escape. Nobody came. In a trice, she decided to bang the bedroom door closed, deliberately hitting my face very painfully.

I was certainly stung to anger as all men must be when their women misbehave. My wife's misbehaviour was particularly outrageous and ridiculous, because her reason for maintaining the darkness was to keep our electricity bill down. If it were not for the flimsiness of this argument, I am sure I would have given her one huge slap. I checked myself: perhaps she was going insane.

'What's the point keeping electricity bills down and medical bills high? What have your budget cuts got to do with giving me punches left and right?' My tone was meant to tell her that my temper was burning red and that any little slip of the tongue might earn her a blaze. But rather than respond, she rudely switched off the light again and sat back in bed.

After taking her time she said, 'You university professors don't pay medical bills. That's state business. You're treated free, spoilt. All I want from you is an explanation why you've come home late.'

'You've no right to question where I have been, let alone what I have been doing there. A man comes home when he likes, his wife wakes up when he comes, opens the door and gives him warm food. I want food right now.' I stressed the 'right now', and switched on the light.

Instead of obeying me, her only husband, this woman switched off the light, sat down and started slapping what sounded like her thighs – as all our women do to display shock. She apparently believed that it was not like me to talk to her so rudely. Yet if this hard talk was going to test her sanity, then let it be. After all, I too had been shocked out of my drunkenness by her behaviour.

I turned on the light.

Not once since our marriage had I beaten this woman. Not because of weakness on my part. No. I believed it contrary to my own modern concepts of marital relationships beating somebody I loved.

Suddenly, I believed it below my dignity as a university lecturer to have my wife howling with pain in the middle of the night. The lecturers next door would hear, and not only backbite but make fun of me in the university senior common room. No, wifebeating would be tantamount to lowering the dignity of the highest institution of learning in Nairobi.

Tonight, however, these beliefs seemed to have been taxed beyond bearing. With this woman behaving like a tigress, I was contemplating doing one thing: expressing my manhood. And the only way this could be done to any hard-headed woman was through very thorough and complete beating. I brandished my fists in her face and furiously chewed my lower lip to bring home to her the mauling that was coming. She was not moved in the least. Instead, her calmness deepened. Her hands stopped their slapping in response to my threat as if they wanted to fight back. She held her chin, resting her elbows on her thighs. She expressed her disgust by click-clacking her tongue very loudly and then pouting her lips as if she wanted to detach them from her body.

This expression was unbearable. No normal Luo woman did that to a husband because it implied that she was accumulating saliva in her mouth to spit in his face. Spitting saliva on a husband's face was such a big curse, he would immediately fall sick and inexorably wither into a corpse. As the saying goes, she had, by virtue of the spitting, symbolically ejected the man out of her body as if he was refuse condemned to the grave. This is why, as I watched those lips pulling themselves out of her face, fear gripped me and my threats melted away. If she did what I feared she was about to do, my clan in the countryside was going to bandy about the saying that I had died 'without seeing my back'. This would mean that I had died without reproducing myself in a son or a daughter in whose back I could see a replica of my own. They would sing their disappointment that I had died without seeing all my sides, that I had slunk into the bowels of the earth without turning my own child around in my arms to admire all the sides of my body, my total life. They'd say I had kept away from the clan because I was barren. Above all they'd argue that I had deliberately provoked my own wife into spitting in my face so that I could die sooner and hide my shame in the grave. I knelt and begged her to spare me this ignominious fate. Her small mouth opened, exposing her small white teeth, and then implored me in a whisper not to genuflect as if she was a god. A heavy sigh escaped me and I genuinely felt resurrected.

'Can't you be ashamed, doing that in this community?' Her tone was confident as if her security depended on the intellectual community around her and not me, her husband. I said I didn't know what she meant.

'Beating your wife or even threatening to.'

On other occasions I would have rudely asked her if I or the community were her husbands, but that night I was a beggar and dared not.

'Let us talk about ourselves and not the community,' I suggested.

'Why should you fear the community as if I have another husband there?' I could hear and feel the suppressed anger in her trembling voice.

When she realised that I was unable to reply she shot another question. 'Have you caught me sleeping with any?'

In the present circumstances, I couldn't possibly tell her that this was not a remote possibility in my mind. Once again, I kept quiet. But poor me, I did not know that silence could talk and say yes and that it could provoke such an angry reaction. She jerked herself up, tore away her see-through nightdress and started wailing, tears flooding her face.

I decided to let her cry her tears to a standstill because I did not know the origins of this state of affairs. I took it that I had interrupted the course of a dream, and that the best thing to do was let it flow to the end. Otherwise I might be damming a river and soliciting my drowning in the process without knowing it.

I let her go on prancing and howling all over the bedroom. I heard her voice getting raucous and the vigour of the drama fluctuating between high and low but no signs of stopping. When her river of tears had flowed to the end, maybe some analyst would look into the water and come up with its chemistry. I heard her and watched her, but particularly watched. All her curves, from neck to toe, were still there. Quite a feast for my eyes, I must admit, and a good diversion from the strange show my wife was putting up. Those curves were still there because she hadn't had a child to disfigure her. 'A child, indeed!' I swore to myself. Immediately after we got married, I swore against having a child for economic reasons. I wanted to live well, save money and enjoy life with my wife without that little thing called a child. That little thing which would come and parasitically nibble our thin purse. When and how would I ever go to the beach for holidays and caress those shapely curves with a greedy child strutting and fretting around for attention! Anyway I loved the curves the way they were without anything between us. Occasionally in the past, when inspired, I would tell her that the world had been a desert until I met her, my throat and tongue cracking with aridity before I sank my mouth into the oasis she carried. I would tell her that I had looked for her shapeliness all over the world, travelling through magazines and newspapers, until, dry-mouthed, I met her. She would reply, with a caressing slap on my back, that, like all poets, I was a liar and a flatterer. I particularly liked the fact that, of all people, she had recognised my poetic qualities. While the whole of Kenya had refused to accord the greatness of the oral poet I secretly believed I was, my wife had. Almost every night since our marriage, I had used all manner of tricks to provoke her into calling me a poet. Then I would feel great and sleep like a lord. Only tonight, of all nights, I was being denied the opportunity to display my poetic genius.

Instead the wailing continued. My inattention had done nothing to stem it. By now, my neighbours must have recorded everything for tomorrow's common-room gossip. That, however, was not my biggest fear now. From the curves to my bedroom poetry, my mind had wandered back to my rural countrymen to comb out what my kinsmen would do to a hard-headed woman like this one jumping all over the bedroom like an unattended cow on heat. My kinsmen would whip such a cow into submission. That's something I had sworn I'd never do. Once I had refused to whack her, my kinsmen would warn me that a woman's wailing had too many consequences to be taken lightly. It was the fear of those consequences which woke me up to the ongoing reality. I immediately felt extremely scared of two things.

First, the consequences of a woman in tears stripping herself. That was the most extreme expression of anger by any woman married in my village, stripping stark naked and wailing in the glaring light. If it had not been for my university education, I'd have thought of this instead of taking diversions into human curves, beach visits and what have you. At least, I'd have known that a moment ago, when I feared her anger had spilt out, this stripping and the intermittent ululations were that anger. The consequences of the anger were grave. This woman was behaving as if she was courting death for her husband. I automatically feared that she wanted me to die so that she could, naked, tearfully mourn me as custom and tradition dictated. I had no alternative but to ask her if she was determined to kill me with her mourning tone. She denied it, and increased the tempo of her antics as if I had fuelled whatever the problem was. She spurted more tears and kicked the air like a wild donkey. I did not make the least move to stop her now that I was assured my only life was out of danger.

Instead I told her my second fear. Having stripped naked in anger, I dreaded what would follow: she was going to stop dead, stand upright, turn her back on me and bend very low, exposing the inside of her thing to bewitch me. Many a woman had done this to her husband in my village. Yes. She was going to destroy my eyesight and mind and blind me for ever. She had already done enough of the forbidden, standing and dancing naked before her husband. When I told her, she confessed she had never remotely imagined she could bewitch me whatever interpretation me and my countrymen might choose to make of her behaviour.

It became clear that I had all along been caught up in a false impression as to the cause of this woman's hysterics. I decided that I was the cause. How I was I didn't know because, as I have said, I was convinced it wasn't my late arrival. Whatever it was, the only available instrument for its solution was myself. It struck me that some reference to a car was necessary to excite and divert her attention from the husband-bewitching statement or whatever else was behind her madness. So in the thick of her physical exercise, I lied that I had seen a beautiful new brand of Peugeot in town, that it was sharp and sexy and that the eight seats were electronically convertible into a treble bed when necessary. I stressed that our car would be a new factory-made thing and not the common second-hand junk university teachers barely afforded from their meagre salaries. It was as if, by this statement, I had added a ton of petrol to a small fire.

She blew up and started jabbering in an unintelligible language characteristic of people possessed by those ever-present ancestral spirits. She jerked, trembled and bubbled with tears and sweat as if she was some widowed woman stung by the latest worm of love recently hatched and released from the grave of a long-dead husband.

I sincerely feared she might run mad. I imagined some kind of therapy or at least a tranquilliser, but there was none close by. I thought of calling a doctor or the sluggish police, but dismissed these immediately because the story would leak to the rumour-mongers and the press and reach all the ends of the world. I fervently hoped that she was not possessed by any anti-Peugeot ancestral spirits because I was not rich enough for the required exorcising ritual.

At the height of it all, I found myself crying and pleading with her to spare me the ordeal. I consciously became hysterical and the higher my madness climbed, the calmer the woman grew. An actor and producer trained in London and Los Angeles, I was putting my education to practical use. It was working. I cried, scratched my hair, bared my teeth and laughed the raucous and guttural laugh of the famous laughing hyena. Seeing the hyena-act take effect, I doubled my efforts. I came to the stage where the hyena has laughed enough and adequately cowed its victim into readiness for a telling bite. A genuinely frightened but silenced heap of human flesh crumbled before me. I calmed down gradually, convinced that a sudden stop might rekindle her drama. As I saw her curve into a comma of submission, I felt an inward triumph of my manly genius and knew this was the appropriate moment to command and demand as I wished.

Standing astride her on the floor I asked for food, but she retorted laconically, asking where and why I had been and didn't make a move to serve me.

I immediately wished one of my ancestors could possess me right there and react to this question. She would have received severe pulping, and that squeaking mouth of hers would have been battered into everlasting silence. Unfortunately my formal education had broken down my communication with these ancestors and I could handle a disobedient woman only verbally, not physically. Unlike some of my colleagues, I was not able to administer the violence they said would tame any woman. I was too 'civilised' for this.

I started off with the lie that I had been watching the flagging-off of the Kenya Marlboro Safari Rally and using the opportunity to select the best car we would soon buy.

'The day you buy that car all the tortoises in the world will buy skirts, wash, iron and wear them. I'm sure I might be a grandmother before I ride even a bicycle.'

A grandmother! As if she had a child already. I steered clear of this issue of imaginary motherhood and didn't tell her that she lacked the qualifications of a grandmother because she would point an accusing finger at me for clinging to the birth-control pills. I withheld this response to her comments to avoid further explosions. I stood her up, sat her on the bed and put my head in her lap.

'Don't lie. You've always hated the Safari and couldn't have been watching it. You must have been carousing somewhere.' Her tone was authoritative as if she had been there to witness what I was doing.

I insisted I had been watching the Safari and selecting our car of the future. I said I only drank a few drops of whisky after making the selection and then hurried to the bus to reach home safely. I thought she'd thank me for taking such good care of her husband, but she didn't.

'Whatever you say, the time you came home tonight was too late for me. Whether you are buying me a car or not, I don't care any more. You have been murdering children in my womb for the last ten years or so that we don't have any to spend money on, all because of a car. Rather than children, we should save and have a car!' The tremor that had erupted into wailing was audible in her tone. I remained silent to avoid another flood of tears. She paused expectantly for a while and then started stroking my hair before coming to a sudden stop. Her face remained calm but she click-clacked her tongue before talking.

'You are greying. I can pluck out a bunch of hair if you want proof. In a week's time you'll be 45 and childless.' I almost cried when she pulled out two strands of white hair and thrashed them in my face.

'I still feel like twenty and poised for more romancing.'

'All you want to do is caress a car. Even when you hold me, it is always to congratulate me for taking more contraceptives in honour of the coming car. We didn't marry to rear a car. Enough of romance. Enough of beach holidays. Enough of wasting time wandering all over the country.' She was no longer talking; she was ordering. When the wailing had greeted my arrival, it was volcanic eruption. Now the hottest after-lava was beginning to ooze out in words. Either it had to be cornered and controlled or it would burn everything I had imagined for the future.

'Dear, a child is for the future. Now is the time to relax.' She eased my head off her lap, slipped into her nightdress and rummaged in the drawer for some underwear. She put it on so slowly I figured that it was less from moodiness than a deliberate gesture to capture my attention. Perhaps I was being too sensitive but it seemed to me that her behaviour was a way of locking her body out of my sight. After dressing, she sat on the bed, speechless for a while.

'I want a child now to keep me company while you are carousing deep into every night. I am not a car manufacturer. I will not stomach the car talk any more.' This was too final to be contradicted.

'All right then, I'll give you a child tonight provided you give me food first. I'm pregnant with hunger.' My light-heartedness was from a feeling of relief that the cause of tonight's chaos had been revealed: a child was overdue.

'It is dawn, close to breakfast. Sleep.'

'I can't with this worm of hunger excavating my stomach.'

'Well, eat your lateness!'

I saw a cynical smile blanket her face. Then she stood up, grabbed the switch roughly and put out the light. I sincerely hoped this was a blackout on our discussions, but particularly in connection with the child. I brushed aside my hunger and religiously waited for her to sink deep into sleep.

Hearing Susan snore so comfortably against my desires gave me the feeling of a hungry expectant husband coming home late for supper and finding a perfectly laid table with ice-cold food as if the wife intended to numb his mouth. On the other hand, why should I rave against her when her inclination to collapse into sleep so fast was simply boosting my family planning, postponing the conception by at least a day! With that I resolved to go to sleep hard.

My slumber was, however, rudely interrupted by a dream. I was driving our car, Susan next to me. A heavy downpour was in progress. Slicks of lightning were flickering all over. Then a brief silence, followed by thunderous roars. Then silence again. But only briefly. When the roaring resumed, a deafening thunderclap came down heavily and smacked me so hard I counted five gory weals on my left cheek with my eyes hanging from my face by thin threads and the car smashed into smithereens. Susan, who had been sitting next to me, was nowhere to be seen. When I opened my eyes, I found her standing naked, next to me, smearing herself with one of the dozen body-oils she used every morning. I tried to pull her to me for a good-morning kiss but she pushed me away, protesting I was wasting her time.

I felt pained and told her. It was curious why she used so much oil as she dressed to go to work. Was she going to entertain her boss and typewriter with her smell? She replied that secretarial ethics required smartness and that it didn't matter whether she didn't allow me to enjoy the aroma through a kiss because the closest I had ever cared to come to her was late every bedtime. She said I could ill afford the time to be with her when she was at her best. I explained it was her work and mine that kept us apart and that a kind of redress was necessary. I made a proposal that all secretaries should dress as well at bedtime as they did in the daytime, if not better. I thought it ridiculous that she should dress so well and beautify her skin for work and not for me.

'You are crazy,' was her answer.

She asked me to do up her zip. I gladly obliged because this gave me a chance to kiss her back despite its oiliness.

Downstairs there was the cacophony of the table being laid for breakfast.

We had strictly instructed the servant never to climb up to call us when food was ready. We had asked him instead to be whistling loudly and continuously until he heard footsteps coming down. This would normally take up to twenty minutes. It did not matter if he whistled longer because we were paying him for everything he did in the house. Three hundred shillings a month and a servant's bedsitter were more than generous to a nonprofessional primary school drop-out with four children and a wife. I had a four-bedroom house on the strength of my higher education. All the same I could not share the house with him because we were not intellectual equals anyway. Furthermore, and as my countrymen believed, if I allowed my servant's kids to live in my house before I got my own I was definitely going to die childless. Moreover his big family was not my business because he had, unlike me, ignored the government warning that Kenyans should not produce children like rabbits. Served him right if his house was crowded.

As we ploughed through the breakfast, I told Susan that she wouldn't be hurrying with her meal if we had a car.

'If we ever have one,' she forced between mouthfuls.

'Yes, we'll need it to take our kids to hospital, school and the parks.' This ingenious combination of children and a car would impress her.

'Now who are these children when we don't have even a foetus? If you refuse to help me get one, I know how to get one myself.'

Her threat was unsettling because it meant either my manhood was dubious or another man was going to impregnate her. I did not ask her about these possibilities because she might have said yes to either one and broken my heart. I was almost playing the game of some lecturers and professors who pretended ignorance of their wives sleeping with men they knew so well. Not that I knew for sure somebody was screwing my wife. No. The problem was the suspicion. Where there was suspicion there were possibilities. Come to think of it, with contraceptive drugs and devices all over women's bodies, how could one trust one's wife completely? She could easily be laid by another man without any danger of pregnancy. The more I thought about it, the clearer it became to me that contraceptives were dirty devices which promoted promiscuity and unfaithfulness on the part of the wife. Medical science was corrupting the world, blocking the womb to enable a woman to mess around. Nobody has told me that my wife was a crook but for all these ten years something might have happened. My people said that when a tree is full of ripened fruit, it is the beauty of their screaming readiness and not the absence of one fruit that rivets the attention. My wife was solidly beautiful with those rippling curves which seemed to move without moving. With this unblemished and seemingly unblemishable solidity how could I know if she had carried a thousand men on her body? I decided at once and irrevocably that I was going to ruffle this solid stuff at all costs. I told myself, as our people do, that the best way to stop foreigners traversing my lands was to create in the centre a mountain nobody could climb. I was going to give Susan a mound to carry. I sat forgetting my breakfast, lost in those thoughts, when Susan rudely asked me to stop dreaming with open eyes. I dived back to the food like a practising hunter sticking his spear in and out of the ground, peeling off slabs of hard rock every time he pulled other spears out unbroken to demonstrate how strong the weapon was.

During the ensuing mouthful I resolved not to go to campus today, to avoid the temptation of visiting the common room for a whisky or two. The university was as usual closed indefinitely after a violent student protest against bad food, dirty kitchens and unwashed cooks, whose stench any healthy human nose could detect a hundred yards away. Most lecturers just reported to office, lied to their secretaries they were going to study in the main library and instead proceeded to the common room where they swigged liquor until dusk. They were lucky because, as they drank and gossiped of the beauty of women's legs and buttocks, or the twenty-year-old research the professor of electrical engineering had been carrying out into the quality of electrons in fish gills, their secondary-school educated secretaries believed that as university dons they were always busy formulating and reformulating lofty ideas for national development.

I was so distracted I couldn't finish my breakfast. Susan had to go to work, and although I had not had a bath, I decided to escort her to the bus. This was perhaps the tenth time in ten years I was affording her this show of affection. She told me she was sweetly surprised and strolled as if she wasn't going to work.

'I'll surprise you today. Just in case you can't push your way into the bus I'll help you.'

'Yes, Henry, by now you ought to have been pushing a heavy pregnant woman into your car.' She said it jokingly, hitting me with the rare smile which always made her small mouth grow beautifully big without being big and revealed her shiny deep dimples.

The rare courage she had to address me by my name was the surprise of the decade, because that was the first time. All the women of my country, including my paternal grandmother, never addressed their husbands by their names. Instead they straightaway said whatever and assumed the men knew they were being addressed. They also avoided the men's eyes. Significantly Susan was staring straight into my eyes as she talked. My instinctive expectation was that she would look away, call me 'Father of My Children' or 'My Bull' or 'My Guardian' or something nobler and then state whatever her mind had chewed over. If my mother had been around to hear her call me Henry and look in my eyes, the old woman would have abused, berated and spat in Susan's mouth and white eyeballs in disgust.

When we reached the stop, the first bus was gone and we had to wait another half an hour.

'I'm surprised you called me by name.'

'You needn't be. Kenya has been ten years independent and things

188

have been changing. This isn't the Kenya of our mothers.' She sounded as informed as a sociology and political science student. She spoke like one of those blasted feminists who didn't know or decided to ignore the fact that God was a male and therefore Man was the legitimate ruler of the world in every sphere of life and must be revered.

I feared she might be getting infected by the Women's Liberation Disease, and deliberately kept silent, hoping she would hop to another topic.

She looked at her watch contemplatively. 'I'm already late. Tell me, hubby Henry, why are we late in everything? We don't have any property to generate profit. Why? Old as we are, do we really have time left?'

This woman had grown too wise and clever.

'Yes. We have lots of time. Some illiterate Kenyans got roaringly wealthy in their seventies. So why not us in our early fifties? You wait till I acquire the PhD. The whole world will come to know me and pour research money into my bank account. I'll prolong the researches into twenty or more years so that I have the time to generate financial profits from investments before writing back to the donors hundreds of pages of verbiage detailing "the initial glimmers of success screaming for further financial support".'

'Even a snail, unless crushed, reaches its destination,' was her comment.

'Even pedestrians go where motorists have been.'

'Today, this morning, I'm convinced you're a verbal fighter. You can defend yourself.'

'I thought you knew that ten years ago. You got married to a man you didn't know well.'

'A mysterious man is much sweeter when broken open as late as I have done it today. In fact I'm beginning to feel so possessed I might not even be able to work today.'

'The bus is coming in another ten minutes. Prepare to wrestle for a seat. Go. Work. Don't be possessed about me at work. Otherwise you might get the sack and nothing to eat.'

'I hope liquor will allow you, for once, to come earlier than me.'

'Me and liquor won't meet today. Me and Susan will meet tonight. We have a date.'

'Sure?'

'Yes a date with a bait called Susan.' I was disappointed she didn't appreciate my poetic lines because she was anxious about the approaching bus. 'And call me,' I added as she shoved her way on.

An hour later she rang and woke me from a sweet slumber in the bathtub. After washing, I had decided to sit in the warm water and reread Mbella Sonne Dipoko's *Because of Women*. I had read a few pages before dozing off. When I woke up, the book had long drowned in the water and the telephone was howling for my attention.

When I picked the phone and automatically said, 'Susan's husband speaking,' she wondered that I knew her before she had even expressed herself.

'What if it had been somebody else and not me calling?'

'Well, there's no harm in declaring to anybody that I'm your husband because I am.'

'But your name isn't Susan.'

'Suppose we overturned things and called myself Henry Francis Susan, it wouldn't change the nature of our relationship. I've read a lot but I haven't found a clause ruling that the husband's name must come last for a wife. I believe it is perfectly in order for me to say I'm Francis the husband of Susan or in brief F. Susan.' Another spontaneous stroke of genius.

She laughed approvingly for a long time before my interruption.

'By the way, a novel I was reading drowned in the tub while I slept . . .'

'That's why you took so long picking the phone.'

'Yes. I had reached the chapter where a man dies because of a woman. He swims desperately to reach her but dies in the process. So you can see I almost drowned for you, trying to find out why you were so harsh to me.'

My reference to the events of last night fell on deaf ears. All I got was: 'I'm sure I woke you up before the final heartbeat. I must have come in the nick of time.'

I paused, expecting more. When nothing came, I decided that it had been her night and let it belong to her.

'You're more than a saviour. I already had breathing problems when I first picked up the phone.' I was lying. My face had been far and safe enough from the water. But I wanted to humour her, a traditional technique for deepening and maddening a woman's love.

'I wish you had been around to save me yesterday at work.' Her tone became grave, close to last night's levels.

'Why, what happened?'

'The Registrar called us − all secretaries − to Council Chambers. He instructed us to get ready for the festivities celebrating the ten great years of Kenya's independence. A long open truck will be provided to the University. All the secretaries are required to board it, with at least one of their kids, and be driven around Nairobi, ten weeks from today. I, the Chief Secretary, will sit at the front with my kid and the driver. When the Registrar mentioned my kid, I heard suppressed giggles all over the chamber and knew they were directed at me. I started crying. When the meeting ended, I flew home in a rage. I wasn't mad with the secretaries. I was mad with you and myself. When you arrived last night I hadn't recovered. But if I had told the story then I'd have broken down forever. I couldn't manage to repeat what the Registrar said about Kenyans displaying soon the fruits of independence they had been nurturing for a decade. What had I grown except our withering selves or is it seeds . . .?'

I wanted to interrupt lest somebody catch her raving about our home affairs. But she didn't let me.

'When I woke up this morning, I was furious with you snoring and smiling drunkenly in your sleep. I felt you were making faces at me as if you were laughing at my misery and humiliation. I gave you a heavy slap as a result. I was actually amused when you woke up and thought it was a thunderbolt.'

'Any weals?'

'No.'

'Well. Don't slap me again. You won't find spare parts for my only beautiful face, so you shouldn't disfigure it. I'm sure you don't want to live with a distorted face for a husband.'

My attempts to make matters light did not work.

'Anyway I was stung by the women's giggles and even when I was in the house, I could still hear their voices pushing more tears out of me.'

There was a long silence before she asked whether I was there.

'Yes, very present and very vigorous,' was my reply.

She laughed, relieving my worry about another verbal outburst.

'I hope you'll be there.' From her tone, it was clear she meant my presence at home. But from the perspective of the arrogant feminists

191

at the senior common room, this expression meant that a man's manhood was absent, not 'there'. The consolation was that my wife was not a member of the senior common room and so couldn't have picked up the expression there. In any case, only university-educated women traded rhetoric about their emancipation. Besides, I believed that my wife only thought and cared for her work and myself and could not be infected by these unarmed fighters. But suppose one of the handful of female professors had been surreptitiously working on her and this expression had actually meant what I thought? After all, she had earlier said that these were not like the times of our mothers, whatever that meant.

I suppressed my fears and attempted humour: 'You'll soon be heavily loaded. By the time of the celebration, you'll be big and heavyweight. I'll teach you how to act tired and expectant, so you don't feel humiliated and left behind. So dear, come here. I'll be here to help you cultivate the weight. When, weeks later, you are asked about your child, you'll have something visible to point at.'

'Something to point at and not talk to could be a stomach overloaded with food.' I wanted to respond, but she burst into such deliciously rippling laughter, I didn't want her to stop. Even when she had stopped and was saying bye, I could still detect crumbs of laughter stuck between her teeth.

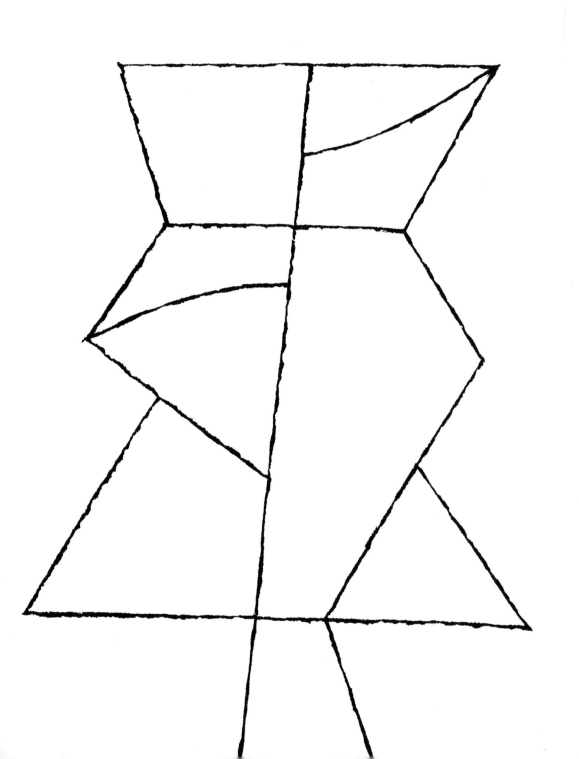

KELWYN SOLE
Go Home and Do Not Sleep

Godukani ningalali, kuz' iziziba zegazi . . .[1]
— Samuel Mqhayi

1

All these many years
I have waited, touch my only

weapon and its tools
with which I stroke the world

its objects amidst
a cloying swamp this prison

where I've waited
earned my jailer's praise
for patience

        knuckles
never clenched to fists
until he could not see

respites given me between
hewing stone recalcitrant

into shapes which might to him
mean something

2

I am behind blade-wire always
peering at the plain
stretching a yawn of yellow gums
to where in the distance

a donga slobbers with its tongue

a path there where my legs
will one day take me swaggering

to loll in hopeful grass
captured by a lone tree's shade
and fall asleep
to prophesy myself upright

and watch
the dusk at length catch flame
the horizons run towards me
on infallible grey feet

3

I can't be seen
until I move

gripping the wall
to you outside
I wave my face
like a handkerchief

4

Tear down the fences:
where they come from:
speak, dance, what you will
                        who now
like I live
in our rulers' dead fantasies

till we wake that final morning

to find prisoners forgotten
clawing up out of the soil
the graves they suffocate beneath,

parting the wire strand by strand
with bleeding hands,

through walls becoming dust
becoming water

shedding their homelands the skin
of their father's orthodoxies,

awoken to move forward
without speech
to no future that I know

5

Until then
I'll stand here

I have those eyes
no one tries to remember

a mouth open
hanging

its portents
only the murdered can recall

1 'Go home and do not sleep, pools of blood are coming . . .'

ARI SITAS
Deaths on the Job
(From 'The Irrepressible Struggles of a Workers' Cultural Local')

On 25 July we had to cancel our music workshop because Miss Petunia McCallum, who was to run it, could not make it to Durban. She phoned from Botha's Hill, from the church retreat there, that she was exhausted; that she had spent the entire night driving a dead man from Botha's Hill all the way to the Hasa area, past Maritzburg and past Howick, searching for a *sangoma*.[1] The dead man, it was confirmed later, was in a bad state — it took three people to hold him down and strap him on to the bed to stop him from assaulting people, and it took two of them to pin him down on to the backseat of Miss McCallum's brown Volkswagen.

Comrade Vusi Maphumulo told me that the man died at Botha's Hill after Dr Philemon Silva got very irritated with the way people would not drop down dead properly during the battle of Mpophomeni between comrades and the *amabutho*.[2] According to him, the situation got explosive and emotional: people chanted battle chants, and danced in the war-style of the *giya* and they were overcome by all this turbulence. But a couple of men, including Petrus Madlala, were playing 'soft': they were not co-operating, or so it seemed. That is when Dr Silva shouted everybody to a standstill and said fiercely, 'When I say *die*, people must *die*!' And shook his fists. Petrus Madlala did. When it was all over, he remained sprawled on the ground. It was Elijah Sibiya who, laughingly, lifted him off the floor, sat him on a chair and stuck a lit cigarette in his mouth, not realising what had happened.

I had met Petrus in the early part of 1987 at Howick. We were visiting the BTR worker cooperatives two years after their strike. The workers at BTR Sarmcol went on strike either at the end of April or May Day 1985, demanding the recognition of the Metal and Allied Workers Union. They were all dismissed and since then they have been struggling to survive and to win their reinstatement. I was part of a delegation of workers from the metal industries of Durban who went out there to visit their cooperatives. And I met Petrus helping with the making of T-shirts in the Co-op. He struck me as a very quiet man, almost shy, a hard worker. He was of a very slight build, with rotting teeth from too much smoking or a bad diet; he was of a very light complexion and he sported a thin little moustache over his cracked lips. We spent a few minutes discussing, out of all things, soccer. According to Vusi Maphumulo he was very malnourished as he ate very little, and the little that came his way in solidarity money he converted to drink. But since his arrival at Botha's Hill his habits were forced to change all over, there was no drink allowed in the compounds and the church people up there stuffed three meals into him per day. He had been complaining of dizzy spells before the incident.

Nobody expected the unfortunate event. That evening Dr Silva terminated the workshop at 9 o'clock. After praising the participants for their performances he asked for critical comment. Petrus complained in Zulu to his comrades that Dr Silva had killed him when he commanded him to die. They tried to ignore the comment, but since it was the only comment being made, Dr Silva asked for it to be translated. Petrus complained to him that when he commanded him to die, he did and he felt his soul lifting out of his body and floating about in the room above the action. Elijah Sibyia, who was always a joker, thought this was very funny and, after retrieving his cigarette from the dead man, he started 'floating' around the room shouting that he was dead. Despite Petrus's insistent comments, everybody thought lightly of the incident and brushed it aside. Dr Silva left Botha's Hill that night pleased about the progress of the play but also uneasy about the death story – he was vaguely worried about the 'strangeness' of what had happened. But he rushed off to Durban for the night because he had classes to teach early in the morning.

Miriam Mdluli told me, (and she is quite close to Dr Silva's lover), that they were disturbed from bed just after midnight by a phone call from Botha's Hill. A distraught Miss McCallum was on the line asking for help: Petrus was beside himself, assaulting people with a metal bedpost he had yanked loose off his bed, screaming after God whom he could not find, whom he could not see anywhere, destroying all the demons who came his way, speaking in tongues and in languages nobody understood. People could not break through his heaven-trance to communicate with him. Three hefty comrades finally tied him down on to the bed and were busy trying to comfort him.

Dr Silva was confused and Miss McCallum was scared. But as they were talking through the wire, word came that Petrus had calmed down. Two hours later, the journey restarted. After a snap debate it was decided that they would not admit him for a mental examination at Edendale Hospital in Pietermaritzburg, but that they would take him to a *sangoma*.

That is how Dr Silva ended up with the murder of somebody who was still alive, Petrus ended up killed but walking the streets, and we ended up with a workshop postponed for weeks.

According to Vusi, Petrus Madlala was 'fixed' by the *sangoma* and by people in the countryside who know about these 'things'; he was last seen frequenting his usual shebeen but he was not in a very communicative mood; he also stopped working at the Co-op. Two weeks later Dr Silva collapsed from a serious ailment that nobody could diagnose – it affected his nerves, his heart, his limbs and his innards.

When doctors failed to come up with something, I and others, realised that we had to write him off.

1 *Sangoma*: traditional healer.
2 *Amabutho*: warriors.

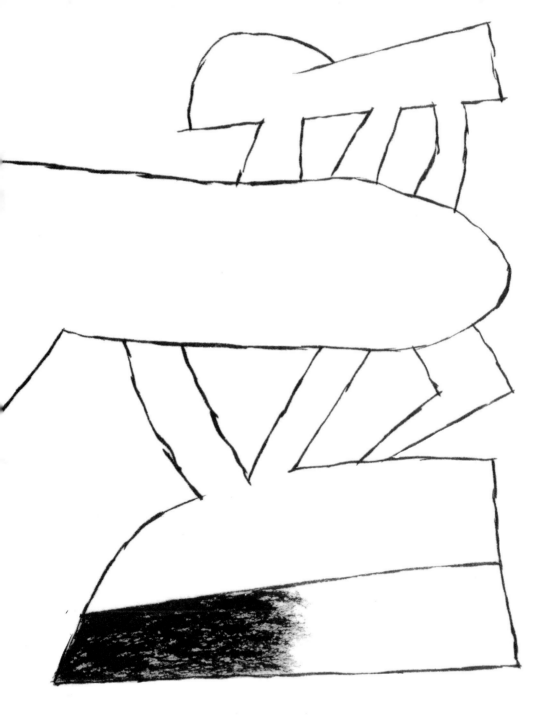

TANURE OJAIDE
The Crow's Gift

Crows now fly overhead where there's bushfire —
they delivered the burnt-offering to the gods
who flushed the earth with sheets of evergreen.
I remember their timely vision and straight flight.

The scar goes back to lick its wound,
the wound brutalises the groomed skin.

How many birds did we break their wings
with the baked balls of childhood foundries;
how many still flew away after we thought
we had tamed them with grains of delight?

When the track dogs of memory
have driven the doe to the marshland,
what happens to the unexpected ducks;
what happens to the fish-ponds
beyond the pale of poaching nets?

I follow birds to their barracks of twigs
where the winged matriarch reviews
the airspace, marks out trails
and beaks out stern orders
to fledgling feathers of the dominion.

Memory, I need no sore knee
for my worship; I need your thread
to lead me out of the dark.

*   *   *

I still cherish the warmth of Granny's back;
she deserves fresh cannons from me.

I cannot tell the way to my father's house;
a wide-mouthed python ran to the marshes.
Whatever studs the orphan survives
in the street of public indifference
help to turn him into a lion's bone.
I prefer to fight through every street
than be smothered in the family home.

I know my relations as a fowl knows hawks;
most couldn't be closer without
the discomfort of bad blood.
Today there is no reason to explain
the earth-sky distance between us,
but the discomfited mouth knows why
it is silent over its scars.

So I always go back but turn from the fire
to where I was refuged like a raw egg;
I have never considered it a birthright
to straddle the blaze of kinship.
O memory, rain a deluge on me.

However credible the creed of adolescent days,
it tears me in one way or the other.
I have reconciled to the people
with whom I share the delta of life.
I can no longer laugh without tears,
nor weep without a smile in the horizon.

How far back can I see in the dense jungle,
how far can I see through the plains

created overnight out of lost territories?
The genealogy of the lion goes back
to cub after cub that grows into a warrior
and disappears in a den of flawless paws . . .

Aridon, give me the crow's gift;
I need fertile grounds for songs.
And let the vision of scars
tear my pathfinding eyes with smiles.

LESEGO RAMPOLOKENG

From an Artist's Notebook:
'Fragments of a Rainbow Revolution'

at the sharp corner moment of castration
at the torment of transition
frozen mid the stride from ash
to finer particled ash
of sand running quick under our nation's feet . . .
at the crossroad
of a sweet load of nymph
turned scythe
above mandela's earth
as he creaks bones to grab a new decade
by its grey beard
there, in the dark of the shepherds flounder
the lamb takes the lead
striding on lightning tread
away from the shepherd's blunder
there, away beware the 'silence of the lambs'
it's the sham calm
between storms

the epoch serpent swift for its old baby age, slipping through society's fingers in disguise.

among the rubble, amid the debris of social stratification of the imperial kind, the sun goes down screaming in the silence of an exploding time. earth gapes, is a wound, and i part of the pus clogging this tormentous moment. i sigh rustling time's bloodied weedblades among the graves of the future. which is here, grabbed between my stubby fingers, burning, sending smoke into my eye, lifted and brought to peeling lips. inhaled, hotly exhaled throughout history.

this is supposed to be prose, not a sorry frustrated attempt at poetry, please get your writing act together writer!

but who decides what what is, who draws the borderline between literary expression and literary expression with a critic's academic impression in a time that defeats metaphor, that no turned and twisted syntax can bind, what critic but the era itself can determine what is good and what bad when notions of bad and good thrash together in some midnight passion breaking sweat on the face of this page.

blood fills my inkwell, i scribble my testimony on my present hammer-and-anvilled flesh. for in the beginning of this story's writing was a lie. a propagandist's ploy to force this time on an ignorant white sheet. spilling bitter and black rumours malicious in their claim to being truthful on your coffee table.

still you tell me this is not a story since stories need lines and threads. blood is a thread. the kind that writes this thing you're now reading.

what's this that you shouldn't tell me what to write yet I must bow down in the manner of its writing?

blood feeding flowers that shoot out of assault rifles of a lie fortified time. beauty amid gore. rosebandages on gorgewounds. birth in the time of genocide. love in the time of hate. growth amid ruin.

the making is in the breaking.

a tap on my shoulder gets me turning and spinning, a mad earth. he's wearing red on his head! the *assegais*[1] pierce my glass. it shatters spilling my thoughts on the floor. but the red is a hat, a sunbleached spotty hat, not a murder band. he smiles at my shocked glazed look and sits down. lines on his face, exile's sandtracks. the wasteland his face my sweaty eyes drag themselves across.

the coffins, two child-sized, they go down and the world is silent, quiet enough to amplify the sound of a teardrop falling with a giddy heated thud into the space between sanity and a time gone mad.

'i'll get you another drink,' he says to my shaking body. my ears hear it but it's some time before it registers. only when he comes back do i hear it brimful. in the beer tumbling down the boulder in my throat. i'm scared. this time is horrors! depression.

this four-year-old boy, this one watching me trying to drink this warmbeer, looking at me from the dusty pavement, he looks blank don't you say, like a judge's signature condemning me to eternal nightmares. he watched his mother pangaed to death, he saw his ten-year-old sister raped and her head bashed against the wall repeatedly until she died after being made to such the cock of a black time. they made him cut his father's throat while they poked a spear into his side as incentive.

when the wind howled it was devil time. light, no, dark rain batted the roof. a woman's voice came out of the dark. asking for help. she was lost, had a baby on her back. when they opened their hospitality the dark night splashed itself red on the wall. relatives took the nervous wrecked boy in. they found him shivering and staring and screaming in the aftermath. every time a car roars past, every time a knock raps the door he screams all hot dampness unleashed and dashes his emaciated body against the wall runs under the bed runs out of the bed hurls himself against the window screaming all the torn and tattered flesh dressed in a natty while. innocence is evil, is matter to rape, to kill. love too. it's dread time.

a man and a woman lie charred. naked and still thrashing in each other's arms long after the bomb exploded at the height of their lovemaking. when it tore them apart it glued them together. carole king was saying she feels the earth move under her feet. they thought the earth had moved for them as well. it had. under their lives. on a booby trapped bed. when they tortured the old bedsprings they detonated the passion of hate. and the death that comes with it.

that boy, his eyes are blank, open, like his mouth, he sits spreadlegged, they tore his anus to thin fleshstrands with spears and knobkerries hanging heavy between the thighs of sodomy. the leader of the packs shouted 'moffieism is not african'[2] and fondled his lieutenant's penis under the table at the next day's press conference. news cameras thought the image best left uncaptured. the blackness wouldn't reproduce. he had drunk of the blood and partaken of the flesh yet belched and said: 'we are defending the honour of the king.' licking the young girl's ruptured hymen off his hands.

every child is my child screams a touched and tortured society. south africa bans the statement as being 'spiritually dangerous' and imprisons its makers. hands them a bible in prison. they read and realise:

god was a hermaphrodite and created adam. fornicated with adam to produce eve. eve's children entered her in a creation orgy to make mankind. the race of man is a result of incest.

216

passion's height, philosophers have called a mini death. the marquis de sade in a mental asylum for telling it naked is testament. bukowski's exploration of the brutality of sex and burroughs's naked lunch eating of doped sex. yukio mishima's stripping and cutting of the veil around homosexuality and dark desires. they bash perversity the hardest who burn in it the hottest.

the healing is in the killing

preachers sneaking off in the dark to indulge in the sin they lambast in others in daylight.

mishima's ritual was pure and complete in his suicide.

and there was socrates executed for blasphemy and daring to make use of his god-given faculties, questioning the holy order. and still centuries later a woman tried and hanged for crucifying jesus christ on her bosom while he screamed in pleasure's throes eili eili lama azavtaning for more.

the imagination is a dangerous place. mary magdalene got paid in shiny pieces of benediction. setting prostitution on sacred ground. but here's a play that puts south african prostitution down to apartheid. ah, how prophets of racial superiority clarioncall it christian doctrined. but there's boredom and sexual starvation, nymphomania. vacuity and the politics of fulfilment. but then again there's deprivation, hunger in the belly feeding hunger between the legs, and deprivation. and then hearts as white as priests' collars' denunciations. millions of dollars, cents, francs, pounds, rands made out of christianity's own brand of religious prostitution in that collection of short stories black bound for marketing effect. necrophilia stands holy in the bible, rape too. the rape of humanity. third worlded countries whored and filled to the wombbrim with acid waste in the rape of man by man, land by land.

dostoevsky brought the soul dirty, bloody, screaming and naked from his underground of worms and snakes and man tied to the hole of unthinking belief to the bubbling hot surface of foetuses burning in the sin. then he promptly died like every unthinking one else. and gogol found refuge from the madness of society by closing the mental blinds on his own madness. and laughed long and loud from behind his insanity's walls. but then there was nietzsche's fascism turning on his mind and feeding off chunks of his sanity. with him hitler mein kampfing in a bunkful of acidstewing corpses, farting hot humanity's mind full of mossgas.[3] on the other hand was van gogh's landscapes falling down on his brains blown to minute brush stroke bits. picasso yielding to the dust thin struggle of mice and cockroaches, vying for foodbits from the table of artless sponsors of artefacts. marx's beard dragging him down to poverty, his face lined with the marks of hunger and his children's philosophy eating starvation to death.

i compose myself like a poem. grey metaphor and white toothed simile. or better still a play. this land is the stage.

one character's only duty is to run around the stage shouting *amandla!*[4] and other slogans throughout. that and the occasional stone throwing at anything that moves. that serves as a breathtaking device. we don't want him to die of sheer exhaustion before the other main character – whom we'll meet in due battle course – gets to him. and of course the mandatory *toyi-toyi*.[5] and then he'll also need an ak assault rifle.

this we'll have to march to the movement's nodding headquarters to demand. for this part i'll need a well *pap* fed soweto youth.[6] ah here's our other main character. what? oh you will need a costume? of course! comprising of only a headband. okay okay you don't need to crack my head with that knobbed-kerrie.[7] a red one, significant of . . .

i see. *okwe gazi el'ghuma li gwaz' inkanyezi*[8] . . . significant of blood. i see.

its letting of course. then he'll need quite a few assegais, shields and knobkerries, demanding therefore a physically fit hostel dweller who knows how to bash something – preferably human – on the head until long after it has stopped moving. he'll need a good voice to shout *usuthu!*[9] at every war dance and head-bashing turn.

side by side with him to add colour to the occasion, i need a blue-clad policeman who won't have a lot to do either. just ride around the stage in an armoured van. shooting directly and incessantly at the youth and his immediate surroundings. then i need a few fire tongued older men to make hot speeches about traditional/cultural weapons. a few skulls with brains – children's preferably, or very weak and elderly people's – spilling out and police mongrels lapping these up will be of some american-award-winning significance. a number of dustbins overflowing with fresh corpses will be of great necessity.

the stage will have to be in ruins, burning, smoke everywhere.

218

the audience will have to make do as best they can. the audience be warned, the likelihood of their joining the cast is very high. throughout the play's run.

insignificant detail cast out, i am also part of the cast, needing to die on the opening night. or day even. or even anytime during the play's run. the time is not set. the dying is, though. this is because i need to dip my finger in my grave wounds to write the script. so i might even have to die before its writing is done. in this event the cast will have to make do on their own. that will not be difficult since the script is written daily across the face of this paper land.

at this point i light a match and necklace a cigarette. the smell of burning human flesh is revolting. but i gulp it down none the less. it is part of the play. he wrinkles his nose at the smell. and lifts his glass to his lips. no! i scream and tear the blood-filled object out of his hand and smash it down on . . . no, before that i look again and find no red inside. he looks at me, a jackboot-puzzled look on his face. after a while, 'perhaps I better go home,' he tells me. where is his home? i don't ask him but the thought jumps out of my stomach and has me running to the toilet before anyone gets embarrassed and moves with the time of my dysentery.

two men, white from the look of them, are on an electric light civilised swear campaign.

'sea kaffir! boat barbarian *pora*.'[10]

'*sout piel!*'[11] one foot in england the other in south africa bleeding penis in the sea!'

we look at them and they turn on us. the rest is best left unwritten. suffice it to say, to write actually, that i thank them here and now for breaking the bones of our monotony. my knuckles are still painful from the flesh encounter. such sweet pain, such painful pleasure.

at the next bar lines are drawn.

'ya the zulus are damn barbaric. all they are capable of is murder and they take that for the height of sophistication!'

'we shall not be led by the nose by compulsively lying kleptomaniac xhosas! *usuthu!*'

'shut up you mountain monkey mosotho, the only thing you people know is eating cats and horses'

'oh ya, when did you ndebele cannibals stop eating human beings?'

'as for you tswanas and your snake skinny pseudo-intellectual sour porridge drunk above the rabble closer to the queen's pink arselicking bullshit . . .'

'stupid like your worm eating ancestors bundu headed shang-aan . . .'

blacker than thou politics in a kaleidoscope country.

'the beautiful ones are not yet resurrected . . . but one settler in one gullet we'll reclaim our history!'

the ultra african comes out from under his grandfather's lice-infested loincloth and adjusts his tie, 'shoo, it's getting hot in wonderland, switch on the air conditioner alice.'

it sinks its fangs into my skull. the fucking awb shitdog.[12] i grab it by the scrotum and javelin it into the air. it yelps human. i jump on to its stomach and blood jets out from between its hind legs. its cry sounds oppressed. i search under my jacket and liquid splashing my face is a furry body dropping dead with a bullet through its head. i kick the hound once more and run as the spca shouts murder!

at the corner a crowd has accosted a man who has just stepped off a train. the gunshots recede into the distance.

'he is inkatha, this bastard. otherwise why should he throw stones at us when we chase him huh, tell us that?'

he is pleading his case against the factional charge.

'you are inkatha swine!'

'no, i'm not, children of my father . . .'

'we are not your father's bastard children . . . okay okay comrades i've got an idea, what is this?' he asks the cringing man, a one rand coin flashing in his dirty hand.

'hi landi!'[13]

'ah ha inkatha!'

the jackal laughter chorus splashes blood and clouds the wretched of the earth man's deathbound screams.

before that in the train the red band burnt his pockets as the toyi-toyi swung with the train's sway. when he got off the train the red band army was on the platform he slipped the band on to his head to ululation. he passed through and on to the street where he slipped the band into his pocket when he saw a group of youngsters milling murder untidily around in the street. but they had seen the band slide in shivers into his pocket. and 'death by ilandi!' the gods of liberation had decreed.

there is a sit-in at the nationalist party's offices to draw attention to demands for a constituent assembly. the women of the land are assembled in their own right or left. on the way there she told journalists as she strung a fur coat across her shoulders, 'i don't have to be poor to be revolutionary.' the meeting is in progress.

'comrades, we stay here tonight! we must all sacrifice!'

her goldtipped teeth shine. a few in the assembly enter into group discussions around the word 'sacrifice'. the ruby and sapphire jewellery around her neck clinks in silver and diamond wristwatch time. in the deep winter night the women watch her fascinated, listening to her satin smooth voice. most tighten their rages around them as babies crying on their backs punctuate the leader's speech. they shiver in the flashing look in her eye and in the cold slithering into their bones. and try to quieten their children. the future lies not in angering your leaders, they know that as deeply as the milk draining out of their drooping breasts on to the hungered mouths of the new south africans on their laps.

long after, they are still there. the songs and dances have died out. the bus to take them back to the squatter camp forty kilometres away has not arrived. the babies scream, the toddlers hold on tight to their mothers' dresses. at that hour, she sips filter coffee and runs her long fingers down and up her thighs, into the silken warmth between, and smiles as a sweet sensation shoots up her spine. the bubbly bath is warm and velvety. she speaks into the red telephone. 'our sit-in was a success, comrade president.'

'good see me at the same time tomorrow and we'll talk about your appointment on to the central committee . . . okay love?'

i reach for my newspaper and 'twenty-eight people died in soweto last night as internecine violence spreads across the reef' another 'coloured people came into being in south africa because european settlers raped our ancestors' the blood curdles 'five more bodies were found in kagiso yesterday following fierce clashes between hostel dwellers and township residents.' as he looks at me a ghostly cloud settles in his eyes. this is a dead time.

bongi menstruated in the week long heat of combat. when the ground erupted and swallowed whole bone and flesh the liquid ran out of her. she used tree leaves for pads. child of an ancient time. the menses stuck blood red to her fatigues. a face as red as the waste between her legs came into her view in her rifle's sights and she swabbed it. another one tried to dive and her bullet helped it on its way. still the waters ran in heavy flow. unheeded they stank the wind. with the leadfilled corpses. shrapnel grazed her thigh and red and red mingled as she fired. the ambush dropped dead. her unit pushed on. war is a reality that knows no embarrassment. no one said anything when after the week she painfully tore the leaves from her legs and washed herself clean in that limpopo of floating memories and corpses.

danger is an aphrodisiac, he tells me. thus they were at the height of their sexual drive when the bullets flew, when the bombs raged. she gave birth in the bush, wrapped the child in an army shirt plucked from a dead guerrilla, after washing it in the drinking water from her canteen. the second child she gave birth to in a refugee settlement makeshift hospital while her comrade kept guard.

in a corner a guerrilla with a fractured leg clenched his teeth tight as his leg was amputated. on another pile of bedding a young child shivered in the grip of malaria fever. some comrades carried out a corpse with its head blown off. the baby was born healthy and fighting fit. she carried both of them across mined ground and back to the plane landing at the jan smuts airport of exiles and guerrillas returning disarmed by leadership and government concord, where the cold blast of june met their homecoming. like the other june that was their exiling. but that was a hellfire burning a path through the jungles of stranger at own home hearts.

it pained him to say it. but he did.

he had never stopped loving the woman he adored before the eruption of winter dried faggots. lena. when he got home she met him with the same fire he'd known years ago. or so he thought. exile has a glamorous stigma. he went home with her. she paraded him before friends she never had when he went away. a few days put paid to it. he walked out and back to bongi and their two daughters. after boiling water arguments taking the skin off his face.

'what hotels did you sleep in in exile what countries did you go to . . .'

after the war, after exile, after armies and police forces and cold dark gunlit days and nights. his leaving blew bongi's sanity to shreds. she didn't know his coming. he went back home in the dark. evading

chants of marauding *usuthu*. his red spotty hat tucked down to his
eyes. he was about to knock when he heard a child screaming its life
away. then the other child joined in and 'shut up fucking shit swine'
completed the troika and doorpiercing screams again made him hurl
himself against the door. it burst open under his weight as bongi
herself screamed. the children were on the floor. one clutching its
throat. when it tried to shout his name blood bubbles bobbed out of
its slit throat pipe and ran on to the dirty skinthin carpet. he felt
stickiness grab his shoes when he ran in. gore everywhere. papa . . .
papa . . . mama . . . the other girl was trying to push her intestines
back into her slashed stomach. he had seen all sorts of death. this
throttled his heart. his stomach constricted as his scream hit the
distant wall. they were all pleading with him. it was in their eyes.
the younger one held her hand out to him. before he could get to her
a spurt of blood kicked out of her throat pipe and the hand fell into
the puddle around her. bongi had missed her jugular vein. hurling
'inkatha' in his face before she passed out.

they took her to a mental asylum. she's still there. he's walking
with me from bar to bar. his gait defeated. but he smiles. making me
see blood in his glass every time he lifts it to his lips.

his voice pierces the gravedark in my brains:

'A drunk pissing on my backwall . . . a dirty child slurping licking
thick yellow mucus squatting shitting on my front door while a dog
gorges itself on the faeces. i stuff last night's porridge and a stray
giant green fly while a cockroach contends for a piece of dirt on the
corner of my lips . . . dragging on a cigarette stub that burns my lips
and dreaming of rice and fried chicken while next door a man
deranged with frustration hacks his family to death to escape the
shame of watching them starve to death . . . the smell of blankets
unwashed of the heave and throb carnality born of the uncertainty of
a coming morning and the heavy stench of nightmare sweated bodies
. . . the sound of gunfire providing background music to the
conception of unwelcome babies . . . the chaos of corrosion in
spiritual denial, the breaking down of morality and building of
inverted value systems . . . fragmentation as order . . . the fear at my
loins shooting through the mouth of the woman gasping in my arms
echoing in a next street rape, death and the stale smell of beer in a
drunken sleeping mouth upsetting the glass on a shaking table . . .
blood and the sweat of labouring fear, arrogance as paranoia's

223

disguise, sex as release of pent up rage, arrested emotion, restless speaking in the sleep of dark corners eerie lit with knife and panga flashes, dreams dressed in streetwalking regalia, the powerful scent of a cowardice's hand pulling the pin of a guillotine, fear in a hand throwing a handgrenade, the blast in deep holed eyes . . . we have become such willing pavlovian guinea pigs we relish our own frying on a political poker. we gorge ourselves silly on the cake of slogans . . . with a fist in the air mary antoinette becomes a south african version of the statue of liberty . . .'

he drowned his tirade when a lone tear fell into his glass.

'are you diluting your beer?' i asked him, wanting to be malicious, aiming to hurt. it hit him. he rose out of his chair. face muscles moving. body clenching and unknotting itself. he needed to let that emotion go . . . before i could steel myself to it, before i could avert the attack or at least block or duck under the blow he hit me full in the face . . . with a smile. i slumped in my chair.

'maybe we should blast a building and claim it's a plot to derail the negotiation process,' he says and laughs dry bones. but i'm not listening to him as matters anti-climax. vultures gather round to pick the fleshpieces of an oppression presumed dead and frying in the sun. man what a con-fusion. as gorbachev perestroikas his shaved off beard, contemplating dividends, the mangy thatcher hawks in and steps on a blood red carpet. then, in the sound of an explosion among cakeplates and teacups the negotiation table in palpitations is struck dumb and unfounded.

i watch the sun go down redtinted golden through the liquor haze of that boy looking at me. he becomes many children as the sun settles in the glass in my eye.

i close my eyes and lift the glassful of fire to my dry lips. when i open them he is no longer there. i blink and squint out into the gathering gloom but he's gone.

i think of the screams and the running and the beds and blood and knocks on the door and cars cruising or speeding past or stopping outside the house or next door and him hitting his head against the wall in this stormstern gloomy time of a rainbow revolution and something hot and liquid falls down my cheeks.

a sudden chill runs up my spine and settles behind my head. this head is a heavy load. i lower it to the dusty ground.

1 Inkatha warriors wear red headbands.
2 *Moffie*: slang for a homosexual man.
3 Mossgas: a controversial state-funded gas exploration.
4 *Amandla*: Power!
5 *Toyi-toyi*: a militant dance.
6 *Pap*: stiff maize porridge.
7 *Knobkerrie*: a round-headed stick used for fighting.
8 Like the blood that erupts to gore the stars.
9 *Usuthu*: Zulu war cry.
10 *Pora*: slang for Portuguese.
11 *Sout piel*: salt penis.
12 A.W.B.: Afrikaner Weerstand Beweging, a right-wing Afrikaner nationalist movement.
13 Zulu has no 'r'. Some Zulu-speaking people would pronounce 'rand' as 'land'.

KEORAPETSE KGOSITSILE
I Am

Beware my friend
I might be millions or more
Things than what you have convinced
Yourself I am
        I am what
            I am

Without apology or hypocritical regret
When sound grabs me
And hurls me into the heat of music
I can be a Coltrane Coleman Dolphy solo out there
And deeper than any word you know
Probing and exploring
Every crevice and slice of life
From now to all pasts
Presents and any plethora of futures
To bring you edibles

I can be tree
Loving branches swinging
In the arms of wind
Luxuriant leaves in their green laughter
With the sun

I could be an infant
Teardrops at the eyelash
Without a word
Challenging you
To name the reason
Behind the tears
Since you say you know it all

I could be maddog willie
Annoyed past any saying of it
By an idiotic question like
Don't you think there is a danger
That the ANC might be misguided
By the Communists

Then I could be the ghoul
In your nightmare
Which hurls you out of bed
And sleep wet with cold sweat
Because you have just heard
That Communists and terrorist monsters
Have taken over the country and they say
The land belongs to those who work it

Of a night in Cape Town
I could be that angry young comrade
Who insists through his liquor fumes
He democratically wants things a certain way
Who insists clean your place first democratically
Who does not democratically realise
His place is not too clean

I could be CAP[1]
Through the tongue of my walls
Saying it is time we took art
Out of the galleries
And on to the streets

I could be that crazy
Little South African poet who insists
That the heights or flights of
                    Artistic expression

Or the depths that any
                    Artistic expression
Might plunge into must
Be dialectically related to
                    Social relevance

I could be Nadine
Insisting that the writer
Must seriously handle language
Through the texture of life

I could be millions of what
                    I am
Just as
        I am
            Just as
                I am

1 CAP: Community Arts Project.

230

VUSI BHENGU, GOODMAN KIVAN, NESTER LUTHULI, GLADMAN 'MVUKUZANE' NGUBO AND NOVEMBER MARASTA SHABALALA.

The Man Who Could Fly

I want to tell you the story about a man who could fly. No, don't laugh! I have not eaten the *ntsomi* root, nor am I insane.

After leaving school I decided to visit my uncle down at Umtanvuma river to assist him with looking after his cattle and to lend him a hand in the mealie-fields, before going to the mines.

Indeed, I strode the hills and valleys until I reached my destination at dusk. Mind you, the countryside where my uncle lives has its own history. No, don't worry, I won't tell you the history of my uncle's countryside, I will get to the man who could fly.

When I was about to enter my uncle's yard what an extraordinary thing happened! The wild dogs were yelling and barking at me in such a strange rhythm I had never experienced before. What frightened me most was how the dogs were let loose and that no one dared to come out of the hut to rescue me from those savages.

Faced with that horrible dilemma, I forcefully entered the yard and what a tussle I had with the dogs! I was pounding, kicking and doing whatever I could to quell the fury of the dogs. Yes, you may laugh! The tussle for power between me and the dogs continued for quite a while. I finally forced my way to the door of the big hut while the dogs were pulling me with their big jaws.

Eventually I yelled for help and was rescued. I asked my uncle why it had taken such a long time and he explained that his country had been enveloped by a cloud of fear because of the vigilantes who were rampaging and killing innocent people. Therefore no one had had the courage to come out into the darkness to look at what the dogs were barking at.

The following day I was in strength to go to the field to hoe. The day was cool and calm. The vultures were gliding high in the sky. Small birds sang sweet melodies.

I began with my job of hoeing and while I was sweating I heard a strange rhythmic noise like the galloping of horses. As I turned my head to look I saw a man running as if he was fleeing the anger of pharaoh's warriors. As I was about to ask who he was and where he was heading to, a horde of heavily armed men emerged, in a violent mood, hunting him down.

'How can this man escape from these savages?' I asked myself coldly. 'Why do they want to kill him?' Seeing that the victim was about to be mauled, I felt a cold chill running down my spine. At that moment the man was no longer running, but just wobbling as if he was drunk.

There was no mercy in the eyes of the vigilantes, as there was no hope in the eyes of the prey. But just as the attackers were assured of getting the victim a miracle happened. The man flew like a bird up to the sky.

You laugh, my friends – but the vigilantes asked their feet to carry them away in different directions. They, too, ran as if they had wings, their weapons scattered all over the ground.

I myself tried to run as fast as I could but I was just wobbling and paddling as if I was wearing gumboots in a mudpuddle. When at last I managed to reach the nearby bush I had to relieve myself.

When I regained my strength I decided not to look and see what had happened to the man who flew to the sky but to go straight to my uncle's house. But when I related the story to them they just laughed and thought I was telling lies. Even the dogs rattled outside as if they laughed at me.

The next day my uncle decided to go with me because he thought that I was lazy or bewitched. Indeed we undertook the journey to the mealie-fields and we saw a group of people yonder the river at the extreme end of the bush. But the man who flew we could not see.

*   *   *   *

On that sunny day, I decided to park my car along the side of the road. Taking my camera, I jumped out. My aim was to take some pictures of that area which was looking more green in that summer season.

I was still looking around when suddenly I heard the sound of voices shouting somewhere in the fields. I took a sharp focus on the spot where the voices were coming from. Not very far from me a terrible thing was taking place. I quickly put two twos together, and realised the situation.

A certain black man was running like a springbok away from a group of men who were chasing him with axes, assegais and pangas.

'Oh, this violence is still continuing. I don't know what's wrong with these black people. Killing each other every day. Just look at those weapons, absolutely dangerous, but all the time they are claiming them as traditional ones. Or probably it's their tradition to use them in killing each other. Just look, they are even shouting, showing that they are enjoying what they are doing. Let me take some pictures. But nonsense! Everybody has seen pictures of this thing all the time in newspapers,' I thought to myself.

When I looked again the men were right on his heels. But then I suddenly saw a wonderful thing which I had never before witnessed in my life. I saw the victim lifting up his body leaving the ground and flying into space.

'Hey, what's happening now?' I asked myself with amazement. But then I remembered that our garden boy, James, was always telling us unbelievable stories about incidents which occurred during their faction fights. He said that they were using some herbs, which they call *muti*, which was preventing them from getting injured by bullets.

'Maybe this is one of those magics!' I wondered, shaking my head. I watched him until he was beyond the hill. 'But why are these fools still running and following him?'

I didn't take pictures of that area after all. I just went to my car and drove off, thinking about what I had seen.

*   *   *   *

'Earth, make me a hole to disappear into.
Things are bad outside!
Holediggers that never sleep, come!
Elephants that grind everything, come!

What is happening in this world?
What is happening in this country?

236

Ancestors, when are you going to remember us?
Because we trust in you.
Do you still visit the Lord?
Aren't you close to Him?
Here we are dying of violence!

My children are finished!
My sisters are finished!
My brothers are finished!
The same thing goes for my wife.

What is happening in this world?
What is happening in this country?

Earth make me a hole to disappear into
Things are bad outside!
Holediggers that never sleep, come!
Elephants that grind everything, come!

Please help!
The spring winds are blowing me away.
Ancestors, are you the same as Noah's pigeon?

Do you still visit the Lord?
Please run and tell Him the story:
You grandchildren are dying!

Hawu! Do you still remember me?
I thought you had long forgotten me!

Please pass my greatest gratitude
To that unseen man!

Now I've got wings!
I am a bird with wings!
Remain behind with your spears!
Remain behind with your assegais!
You satans with degrees!
You holediggers who never sleep!
You elephants who grind everything!'

*   *   *   *

I was walking through the fields when I heard a voice calling me. It was my boyfriend, Mpo. I asked him why he was running and he said that the vigilantes wanted to kill him.

I called him to come to me so that we could pray together. I believe God is going to help us when we look in His face. And so I started to pray and called His name: 'God please help me and my boyfriend! You've got the power and no one can help me in this case except you! Please enter my heart and my boyfriend's heart and dwell.'

The next minute my boyfriend flew away to the sky and disappeared. The vigilantes came over to me and asked me what had happened to the man who had been with me. And I answered, 'He is in heaven. If you want to follow him you must pray to God. He is the helper.' The vigilantes were too scared to say they were trying to kill my boyfriend. So they started to ask me how to pray to God and I explained to them that God said, Thou shalt not kill. So they must not kill each other. They kept calm and were so amazed about what had happened in front of them and they also heard my preaching.

Then afterwards when I was still praying, and after the vigilantes had gone into the bush, I saw my boyfriend coming back. He came to me and he also became a born-again like me because he saw the power of God. He explained that it happened like he was dreaming. He praised the Lord and thanked Him.

*   *   *   *

'I think everybody is ready for action as we are hiding here. As soon as we see him walking there along the road, we immediately attack him,' I said with anger, reminding my group.

Mpungose whispered that he wished the man had already approached because he wanted to stab him several times on that big mouth he's always shouting with, boasting around.

'O.K., let's wait and see,' I responded. A few minutes passed by and on the road we saw him walking.

'There he is,' nearly all of us said simultaneously and jumped off, running towards him. He glanced behind and saw us. No one told him what to do.

Dube, an old athlete even during our youth days, was running closer and closer to him.

'You catch him until we arrive!' someone shouted among my group. 'Hhewuuuu . . . today is today!' some of us were shouting.

Dube knocked a stone and fell down. I cursed him inside my heart but he quickly stood up and tried to run again. But he suddenly stopped and looked at his weapons to make sure that they were all still with him. Not taking any care of him we passed by. But very soon he was amongst us again.

Our victim was now getting tired and he was shouting, asking the animals of the field for help. We also shouted, calling him to stop. But he never did.

We were just really close to him, when he suddenly did a wonderful thing. He lifted off his body and flew into space.

'Habe, what is he doing now?' I asked loudly and we all watched him flying higher and higher.

We were still confused, when Ngcobo, a short coal-black bald-headed man whom we had left some distance away, reached us. With great anger he shouted to us, 'Hey, *madoda*,[1] this donkey thinks that he knows, let us follow him!' He said that and took a small bottle of *muti* from his pocket. He shook it and poured some of its contents on the ground. 'He is going to come down here again, I'm telling you. Let's follow him.'

We didn't say a word but started running after that bird-like man. He flew beyond the hill. We ran also towards his direction. Beyond that hill we found him hanging on telephone wires.

'I've told you. You see where he is now? Not very long and he will be on the ground again,' Ngcobo said with satisfaction.

We shouted, calling him and swearing at him. Then a man with tools arrived and stood at a distance. We didn't bother him. But when we saw the police van approaching we dispersed.

*   *   *   *

When I was a child, here in this place, people used to fight and kill each other. These wars were caused by arguments or fights between people who believed different things.

One day the war was on in our area and people were dying like ants. My family and I decided to leave the house that night and go for hiding in the forest. At sunset we started our walk to the forest where we were going to spend the night in order to survive. On our way I got lost from my family. This was a hard time for me because I couldn't call their names as my shout would fall on into the wrong ears, that is my enemies' ears. They would catch me and kill me like an ant.

I was so tired of walking and I ended up being fast asleep in the middle of the forest. My first night in this place was so bad, as I had never slept in the forest before.

By the time I woke up, the sun was high up in the sky. I was so frightened when I thought of those killers that if they saw me sleeping there they would have killed me. 'But my only worry was the separation of myself and my family.

I started looking for my family. I looked and looked but couldn't find them, even when I went to look for them at home there was no sign of them. I felt very bad because I didn't know what had happened to them. I left my home to carry on searching for them in other places. When I was a long distance from my home, I saw a group of people making a circle like a kraal.

I realised that they were part of my enemies, and I prayed as I was sure that that was my last day. That day it wasn't a sunny day but I felt hot and sweaty like I couldn't believe. I saw the earth becoming small like a fish can, that time I just thought of death and nothing else. While I was still in that state of confusion I heard a voice from the sky, it said to me that I mustn't be frightened. Even though I heard that promise, I didn't believe that I was going to survive as I was facing death. These people were coming closer and closer to me and I knew very well that I was going to die.

When they were only metres away from me something unbelievable happened. A strong wind blew all over the place and these people were blown backwards, their weapons were thrown down. I felt as if something lifted me up to the sky.

After that I can't tell you what happened because I was like a corpse or a fainted person. Yes, I flew like a bird that day. But I did not enjoy myself because I was not conscious.

Slowly, slowly my memory returned as I was still flying up in the sky. When I looked at myself I realised that my head was facing downwards and my feet upwards, I was going down to the ground. When I arrived on earth I felt that someone was catching me and placing my feet on the ground. As I came down I realised that I was at home. I saw a lot of changes, like trees and grass, and it was clear

to me that I had been away for a long time. I had long forgotten my
brothers, sisters and my parents.

When I got home, my whole family was shocked, they all ran
away from me except my mom who just came to me, touched me
and realised I was not a ghost, I was still alive. They only believed
that I was their brother when they heard me talking to them. My
family was so excited and surprised when I explained what had really
happened to me, about my flying. They gave me a warm welcome by
organising a big party for me where they slaughtered a cow. They
invited all the relatives and we had a nice day together.

*   *   *   *

One day I was called for a faulty telephone wire in the township. As
usual I took my record book and toolbox together with my mobile
receiver and left in my bakkie.[2]

When I arrived I found that up on pole number 2234 a man with
wings was hanging. Down near the pole was a group of men with
dangerous weapons like pangas, axes and spears. I was frightened but
I also felt irritated by the extra work: the man with wings was
destroying telephone wires with his weight.

I felt cold all over and my feet and hands would hardly move to
stop the bakkie. I stopped the bakkie quite close to the group and
with eyes wide open from fear I asked, 'What happened to that half
bird and half man?'

One of the vigilantes answered in a harsh voice, 'We don't know.
Go and ask Unyoko, you blerrie fool.'

Looking fearful at the assegais made me keep on praying for my
stomach which I considered as a first and soft target.

Suddenly the man hanging above us shouted in a crying voice:
'Hey, I am better off here. I'd rather be killed by telephone wires
than by cowards and fools.'

I was confused and frustrated but managed to drive a little further
on to the telephone booth. I took out my mobile receiver and phoned
the manager. I took my time explaining the situation and problem to
him but he just said, 'I know it is a Friday today but it is too early
that you are so badly controlled by alcohol, the way you behave, man.
Vusi, I have no time to be wasted by you. Get up and fix the lines
before it is too late. There is no man with wings and there are no

vigilantes there! Start your work and all the vigilantes will run away and the man with the wings will fly away. Good luck Vusi!'

I was very frustrated. When the manager put down his receiver on the other side I sat down, with tears hot in my eyes. He was so free that he could not understand my problem.

Three children came around. I heard them loudly saying, 'Hoo, what happened to the big bird up there?' One child screamed and said, 'What kind of bird is that, it looks like a human being.' Another one said, 'Hey forget about the bird, what about those *impis* with pangas and axes, let us run away.' They ran away quickly.

One of the vigilantes said harshly, 'Zakewu, Zakewu, drop down from the tree.' The joke was quoted from the Holy Bible but by a vigilante, it was another case.

I thought to myself that maybe I was asleep and dreaming.

Suddenly, a police van came fast in our direction with dust from the street flying up. I do not know who called the police. The weapons were scattered all over the streets as the vigilantes were running away as fast as they could.

A white policeman asked me, 'What is taking place here?' I answered, 'I do not know. I came here to fix a faulty line! When I arrived I saw a group of men with weapons and that man up there with wings.'

Another white police directed his question to the man up on the lines. '*Wat makeer met jou? Wat is jou naam? Is jy 'n man of 'n dier? Praat, jou donner.*'[3] He then took out his gun and pointing it at the man shouted, '*Praat man, of ek maak jou vrek.*'[4]

I came to my sober senses and went out of the bakkie to listen to the story. The man on the wires looked down and cried loudly. He pleaded, 'Help me down and I shall tell you the whole story.'

After some argument, one of the policemen, a short fat white man came out fast from the van with a saw and angrily began to saw at the pole. When it fell over he said, '*Kom hier, the job is klaar.*'[5] The man fell down with a thud, and feathers from the wings scattered all over. The policeman took out sjamboks and gave the man a thrashing.

The weather changed suddenly, and it became cloudy but with some rainbows.

This story was written during a creative writing workshop run by Astrid von Kotze. The authors were students of a course run by the Culture and Working Life Project at Natal University. Von Kotze provided a skeletal outline of the plot and the authors wrote different 'parts', which were later combined into a single narrative.

1 *Madoda*: men.
2 Bakkie: light pick-up truck.
3 'What is the matter with you? What is your name? Are you a man or an animal? Talk, you idiot.'
4 'Talk man, or I'll kill you.'
5 'Come here, the job is done.'

FRANK WILDERSON
25 December 1986. Tangier, Morocco

When the morning ferry's foghorn beats down the dawn he's already poking about for half-smoked cigarettes. By the time the first prayer is over he's seated at a sidewalk café. A talkative kid (today he is twelve) but right now he's all ears. He's hungry, but still he's all ears; open to tales of politics and lust from rug merchants at the next table. When the merchants leave to open their shops he darts to their table and drains the dregs of their mud-thick coffee. Now is his quiet time, this interlude between the merchants' breakfast and the tourists' lunch, time for the fruits of his early morning harvest: He inhales the stale smoke, he ponders and plans.

The ferry pulls away from the pier, its foghorn tugs at the base of his hollow stomach. He wonders what children in Spain and Gibraltar are doing right now. *How do they find cigarettes? How do they find food? Are they as lucky as me, free to come and go as they please? One day I'll pool my dirhams and cross to Gibraltar for a good looksee.* But now, the plans of the day are upon him. Before the sun sets he must line his stomach with more than smoke and coffee.

The British hydrofoil slices into port and he's the ship's captain for a moment too long. The stub burns his fingers, his trance is singed. *Those ships will do it every time!* He lights another, and with deep satisfaction, inhales his good fortune: Tangier is an international city and I have smoked behind half the world.

Two Frenchmen stand before his table: quite tall and blond. They throw down a crumpled ten dirham note, knowing it will lead them to a good restaurant, good Maghrebi cuisine, though not too expensive, and afterward a very good time. He prances down the street leading the way, making them laugh with spicy ribald jokes. For his excellent French they give him more money.

He waits outside while they eat, examining the various shades and wrinkles on the face of King Hassan. When the Frenchmen finish their meal he folds the King back into his billfold. 'Now for that good time,' they say.

'That's ten more dirhams, ten dirhams apiece.' (He tries to make them understand, 'ten dirhams apiece, ten dirhams apiece,' but they are pinching tears from his flesh. He can hardly speak for the pain.) He leads them to the restaurant's alley — 'Ten dirhams apiece, if you please messieurs.'

Thrust against the wall, his world is enveloped in night as they hike his djellaba over his head. He lowers his drawers for them ... drops to his knees ... turns his behind up to the sky and fights back an ancient cursing that is not his, still it rises from his throat until the second one withdraws.

In the evening, after the last prayer, he has his own table, his own bowl of couscous, his own cup of mud-thick coffee. He digs into his pocket and lets his last dirham unfold on the table. The King's face is still faded and wrinkled, in need of starch and ironing.

Beacons of light from passing cars splash his face: yellow beams on eyes of jade, colours too wonderful to live.

He smokes his last cigarette and adds two Paris business cards to his wallet's bulging collection, the way kids in Ohio add baseball cards to shoeboxes.

The moon pours crushed glass into the Mediterranean.

The ferry is just one more light winking on the slope of the earth.

'What are the children in Gibraltar doing?' he whispers into his neck. Then a sharp curse of pain. The stub, the bastard, burned his finger again.

'Who cares what they're doing? Who cares about Gibraltar? I know Tangier like the back of my hand. And I know Europe even better than that boat.'

EVELYN HOLTZHAUSEN
The Voyeur

This attitude of woman, freshly showered,
towelled dry, windmills
up an arm, applies a hiss of spray,
winds down, turns the other way.

The sight of surface nakedness,
voluptuous flesh, breasts,
the tuft of pubic hair:
A voyeur's vignette, indifferent to my stare.

Frantic gusts of winter wind whip
shards of rain to scratch
against the window pane:
Excite surburban lawns to erupt in flood.

She folds down, snakes into a dress
shrugs, reaches back
to seal a mesh of zip,
then strides, preoccupied, into the next room.

A scented spice of woman lingers in the air,
and seems to carry insinuation,
as vague as loss, like water
permeates a film of wet this side of cold glass.

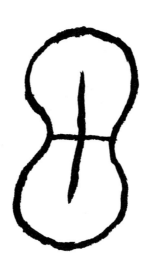

STEPHEN GRAY
Letters to Pratt

Not that he stood much chance of getting away with shooting the prime minister.

The facts of the matter are as follows: on Saturday 9 April 1960, during a cup-giving ceremony at the Rand Easter Show, which in those days was held at Milner Park in Johannesburg, David Beresford Pratt, who was in the member's enclosure because he was exhibiting his cattle, did 'wrongfully, unlawfully and maliciously attempt to kill and murder Hendrik Frensch Verwoerd'. That is how the charge sheet describes the crime. This crime Pratt committed by pulling out his revolver, approaching the seated official party and shooting Verwoerd, the prime minister, in the face.

The photo of Verwoerd going down is horrible indeed. Incredibly enough he survived the bullet, which entered by his nostril and completed its passage by going round the inside of his skull. Pratt was the one who shot him, there was no doubt about that. But the unfortunate Verwoerd had several more years in power to go before he was finally assassinated successfully.

After his attempt on the prime minister's life, Pratt did not have many months to go. He was immediately held in detention under the new emergency regulations. So severe were these that until he was finally charged he was not able even to consult with his lawyer. He was visited a few times by the daughter of his first marriage and by his only other close relative, his sister in Cape Town, to both of whom he was allowed to write a weekly letter about his life in prison — one would pass it on to the other.

Pratt had a bleak style. One such letter reads as follows:

6.00 a.m.	Dress and clean up call.
7.00 a.m.	Wash.
7.30 a.m.	Daily chores.
8.00 a.m.	Thomas à Kempis and meditation.
9.00 a.m.	Exercise.
9.30 a.m.	Read Knox.
10.30 a.m.	Letters.

11.30 a.m.	Chess.
12.00 noon	Lunch and exercise.
1.30 p.m.	Read light literature.
2.30 p.m.	Chess.
3.30 p.m.	Read Therese.
5.00 p.m.	Thomas à Kempis and thought.
6.00 p.m.	Missel.
7.00 p.m.	Read Knox.
8.00 p.m.	Chess.

Love,
David

Another is in sonnet form, ending:

Vain desire and self love hath no place
Upon these pastures reached alone by grace.

He kept all the letters he received, although these were rationed out to him at the rate of a small bundle a week. One of these was usually from his mistress, who lengthily described how she would now have to get a job unless he could help her out. Since his assets were frozen, he was unable to satisfy her requests, but he nevertheless kept all her pleas in a waiting file as if he would fix her up when he could.

With incoming letters so limited, David Pratt could have had no real idea of the impact of his case in the outside world, which of course he would never see again. Also, everything he received was censored with a purple stamp obliterating any political reference he might have been able to use in his own defence. In an extreme case, part of a paragraph would be clipped out with scissors. Where this is really bad you would think the censor was some child trying to turn Pratt's letters into lines of cut-out dolls. If Pratt had lasted to Christmas he could have used his correspondence as decorative streamers.

At any time, the point is that he never knew that the boldness of his deed, which made headlines around the world, among many other things had unleashed a wave of fanatics who bombarded the prison with fan-letters addressed to David Pratt, Esq. They came from all over, in different shapes and sizes. None of these fans was known to him, yet they all had this characteristic in common: each wrote to him as if they had known him for years. I am talking about hundreds of letters a day arriving at P. O. Box 410, Pretoria, with their brown 1d. stamps of a wildebeest of the old Union of South Africa, soon enough to become Verwoerd's Republic. Most of them were from lonely women who admired the dashing, handsome cattle-breeder of the press photos and sought to cheer him in the solitude of his cell. Some men wrote; an example is an old school friend who had decided (or been instructed) not to mention too specifically the circumstances in which Pratt found himself:

> I returned to Natal to find the sardines had at last arrived and we had one of the best runs we have had for years. We netted 20 tons of sardines, and other netting syndicates did equally well. The sardines have never been as late as this but the delay was good as it kept the crowd hanging about so the pub did well. We had the most terrible seas last week and our nets were badly damaged so we are busy getting them repaired. This is the first trouble we have had for a long while.
>
> I suppose you do find time drags terribly – I hope things are brought to a head soon for your sake.

There are many such letters from family, friends and business associates, none of whom seem fully able to grasp their correspondent's dilemma: Pratt was awaiting trial on a capital charge with every likelihood of being found guilty.

His most faithful correspondent was one who first signed the name R. Malan and only several letters later with the less formal Rita Malan. What makes her correspondence so extraordinary is that it appears Pratt never replied to her. Probably his weekly allocation was taken up with business affairs and pressing personal demands, particularly when his second wife returned from Holland to get things straight for the sake of the two children they had together. Yet Rita Malan persisted, in the hope that one day she would receive a response.

> Dear Mr Pratt, you don't know me from a bar of soap and most probably you never will, but I just want you to know that while you are 'inside' there is someone outside who thinks all the best thoughts for you. Your sincere admirer, R. Malan.

Dear Mr Pratt, Last week I wrote to you. You can tell it's me by the light blue Croxley, which must remind you of the colour of the sky, and the terrible handwriting I have, which this nib only makes worse. I know from my son who is a prison warder (but not at your prison – he's in Barberton of all places) that you may receive limited letters. Where he is they don't give out letters to the blacks at all, but when you're expected to be on death row you do get some. I say this just to lift your heart. An admirer, yours sincerely, R. Malan.

Dear Mr Pratt, This is your admirer again, and you must be wondering who I am and why I so admire you! Well, it isn't just your good looks, you know, and anyway I'm far from being one of those teenagers who just go mad over some movie star's picture. But I have collected every cutting there's ever been on you, and so from my scrapbook I have learnt a considerable amount: you inherited a sweet factory on the Rand which is the basis of your fortune; your fine education, marred only by the blight of epilepsy; playing polo and all and your fine war record in North Africa and Italy. And how you tried to run for the UP in Magaliesburg where you have your ranch and the first trout hatchery in South Africa too. I gleaned it all from the papers and from your manager; they keep the place in model condition. I went out there to do some research on the ground, as they say.

Soon you'll be able to say a year, a month a day . . . and I'll be able to say in 1959, 16 May at 12.00, David Beresford Pratt did this. Well, on that day you were having a secret lunch with Dr Dönges, weren't you? – putting your money behind a secret plot to get rid of Verwoerd before he brought the country to ruin. By 1.00 p.m. old Dönges had walked out, and so had the other very powerful man: Diedericks, wasn't it? They both walked out, but they didn't tell on you to the police, did they? You see, I have done my detective work. I reckon if you couldn't persuade them to stop him by normal means, you thought you'd have to take on the burden yourself! Am I right? You know you didn't have much time anyway, so why not take him with? Yours, Rita Malan.

Dear David Pratt, Forgive my familiarity, but I get to know you more and more. I feel as if I know you, even though we've never met and never will. But there is so much to say in your defence and now you say in the paper you will have no legal team, but will defend yourself. (This isn't said directly because you may not be quoted.) You *must* have defending council, because they want to argue under the Mental Disorders Act, No. 38 of 1916, that you were partly incapable, therefore while of unsound mind you committed or attempted to commit a crime for which you had diminished responsibility – and that way get you off, don't you understand? If you defend yourself you'll be guilty and you'll hang. Oh David, please understand this crucial point . . . Or maybe I don't know you well enough after all, and I've not fully registered how you refuse to hide behind anything crooked. Of course I see it now: if you take full responsibility it means you thought that evil man deserved to die; that you *did* mean to kill him [The rest is cut.]

Dear David, I want you to know what very good progress I've been making in unravelling your case and in coming to an understanding of you. I don't think in many details I have been wrong, have I? I found out this terrible story of how you walked into the Magaliesburg pub and called them all Ku Kluxmen and racist bigots and all; well, I've never been into a pub like that, for obvious reasons, but I can just imagine – and you're right of course, these bloody Nationalists will stop at nothing now. So they string *you* up from a lamp-post, a white man, and set your truck on fire and shoot at the support for your feet until you're hanging. They said they put your hands inside the noose so you could stop yourself being strangled. No wonder you hate the bastards! They'll make you swing again, because of what you did to their Nazi leader: so please my [Cut out.]

Dear David, When I sign 'Rita' it means that's my full name – it's not an abbreviation of a longer name. All the women in your life have had such romantic names – but here am I, plain Rita. 'Mrs' of course – I told you about my son. My husband is dead now, so it is just the two of us to make do, and since my son is in Barberton I rarely see him nowadays. You must miss your children a lot. I know your daughter from your first marriage and you were getting very close when this occurred. Her affidavit before the court says this, when she got custody of your financial affairs. She seems a very sensible girl to me – not a spendthrift like some I know. She pleaded very calmly and logically and made a great impression on the judge. Oh yes, I was there . . . how else would I know those details? The courts are about the only place left in this whole country where a person like me may freely go these days. I suppose now he's got a bullet in his brain (thanks to you!) Verwoerd will try and segregate the courts too! Yes, it's true, there is nowhere a person like me may go any more: bioscope shows, out of bounds; no bus to get to the cinema anyway; no books from the public library any more; no place to stay (thank God my old employers keep me on in the back and I go out to char from there). Now there's a curfew and soldiers in tanks, man. To get to the courthouse I had to show my pass three times and finally say *my boss* had sent me with an important message, otherwise they wouldn't let me in as myself – a respectable coloured woman of a certain age. What have I done to Verwoerd that he makes my life a misery like this? You were perfectly justified to act as you did. God made a mistake when He let him recover, if you ask me: xxxxx xxxxxxx

. . . this weekend and my son came, so I feel a lot better. He says even in Barberton even the short-term prisoners are on *your* side. So you're quite a local hero with the black people, my dear! – if you don't mind me being so forward. I don't mean anything by it except to cheer your spirits, as you know. But my dear David, sometimes, although I know I shouldn't, I do wish for a sign from you; some indication of message received. If you get this at all it is only through the ingenuity of my son who is in the prison service and knows how to get these through. Otherwise they'd end up in the rubbish bin like all the other unwanted post and a lot else besides. I don't want my feelings for you to be reduced to ash, at least until I *know* you know of my concern for your well-being.

So let's change the subject a bit: I must keep you informed with all the great events surrounding your famous case. I'm sure you don't know half of it. For example, did you know the night you shot Verwoerd, in the Rand Club (not that I'd be allowed near such a precinct) there was rejoicing until 2 a.m. and you were the toast of the town. Also at Wanderers and Inanda Club (out of bounds to the likes of me). They'd all assumed Verwoerd was point-blank dead. They must have been truly shocked when the *Sunday Times* came out with the news that he would pull through. And I'm now embarrassed for my country, like them, that we have to have this man pull us all into the dirt.

I cannot explain, but I have arranged for a message from you to be delivered to me. Please acknowledge receipt of all the endeavours I have made to understand your case and the esteem in which I hold your suffering. Yours sincerely, (Mrs) Rita Malan.

Dear David Pratt, No sign, no message. I have waited over ten days. The post from Pretoria to Primrose, Johannesburg, does not take *that* long. What am I to say, what am I to do? If you do not wish to encourage my communications, you could not have found a crueller way of saying so. I paid £2.10s., damn it, and unlike for you, for me money doesn't grow on trees. My costs in this case already amount to a small fortune. My pension money's all gone on the room and food by the 20th so what extra I get has to tide me over, but it isn't much. Damn it, you could have given me a sign. Or do you also consider me too beneath you to be bothered about? Yours in true mortification.

All right, I've calmed down now . . . because, well, what else can I do? I have had to decide how to interpret your silence. I have had to face the very really possibility, as well, that you *cannot* in fact communicate with me. My son says, down a long line of hand-to-hand stuff (it is not easy to get from Primrose to death row), that your old malady has reasserted itself and all you do in your cell is sit cross-legged and answer no one. He found out your glasses were broken when they beat the hell out of you, as they caught you when Verwoerd fell – and his security chief got such a fright he *fainted*! – remember that! They dragged you behind the tent and smashed you up so badly they wouldn't let anyone see you for the next two weeks. Your vision is still impaired in your right eye, hey? Maybe you get all my letters but just can't read them properly. DAVID I PUT THIS IN CAPITALS: YOU ARE NOT ALONE. MORE THAN HALF OUR COUNTRY AGREES WITH YOU. IF THEY HANG YOU, THEY WILL BE HANGING ALL OF US. LOVE, RITA.

Many of Mrs Malan's fervent letters to David Pratt included pertinent detail about the events leading up to the assassination attempt: the massacre of resisters at Sharpeville on 21 March that year, the two grand marches into Cape Town of the PAC and the subsequent devastation of Langa and Nyanga, the declaration of the state of emergency in most urban magisterial districts by which any tactics were admissible to stop the stayaways and drive the workers back to work. None of this could Mrs Malan have witnessed at first hand, but that did not mean she was unaware of the reasons for mass revolt, nor disassociated herself from it.

Most of this is cut from her letters. Only snippets remain. 'I wish I could send you a photo cut out of the newspaper of brave Chief L. burning his you-know-what' (Luthuli and his pass-book). 'I wish I could show you S. going to jail' (Sobukwe). The scissors cut out all the main events of a terribly disrupted year, during which apartheid strode in as overseas investment strode out. The scope of Mrs Malan's concerns was reduced by those scissors to her more conventional sympathy for the prisoner.

But one wonderful letter got through intact.

My dear David, I imagine you are over your epilepsy altogether, cured as you never could be in this world, cross-legged on your institutional bed with your hair shaven as it must be. I want to talk with you quietly about the sadness of South Africa now and share with you from my heart what we outside are going through. You probably knew it was coming: this referendum over whether we should have a republic or not, with obviously guess-who as executive president. You and I have one more thing in common now: you as a classified criminal and me as classified 'non-white' will not be asked to vote on the outcome. Nor will most of the rest of our country. Can this really be true that an issue concerning each and every one of us is not even to be put to the vast majority? White adults will decide if we are to stay a civilised nation that can hold its head up in the company of the rest of the world, or a little white state in which no one counts but the Afrikaner. I know how incensed you must feel: for if they win their white supremacist state they will surely be expelled from every forum of this day and age, and we with no choice will have to be expelled with them. I never mind the Queen on our stamps; she makes me think of all the millions of other people of colour around the world who share her on their stamps as well. And now, no permission given by the likes of you and me, we shall have Verwoerd on a stamp, so ungracious, like a great fat pig. And he rules by the will of only 9% of the people! At least everyone had a little love to spare for the Queen, don't you agree? I just thought you should know this, my dear. People will remember the sacrifice you made, even if everyone tells you to the contrary, and even if to you it now sounds so useless. With respect and affection, as ever, Rita.

The last letter Rita Malan wrote to David Pratt he never received. The date of the Primrose postmark records that it was posted a few hours after his death and it would take several more days for the news to be released by the prison service. In her search for a sign, this was surely it. We may reconstruct: shortly after receiving the letter quoted above, Pratt rolled his sheet into a rope and tied it around his neck, tightening it through the bars of the headboard. Once he had twisted the sheet sufficiently to strangle himself, he managed to turn his body around two more times to make the knot even tighter and finish the job.

In other words, having lost out on every aspect of his plan to halt the rising tide of South African racism, he still reserved the right to act on his own behalf before his own life was taken from him. Many of those who remember Pratt still feel that he was murdered, as even a fit and physically tough yogi like him could not have contrived to end himself in such a bizarre way.

Here is Rita Malan's last letter to Pratt, never read by him. What became of her subsequently is not known. As she was elderly then, chances are very slim that she could still be alive thirty years later. Others involved with Pratt are still very much alive, so obviously one has to use discretion in presenting the papers he left behind. I have mentioned letters of family and friends, but none of them seems to register as well as Rita Malan the full impact of how he stepped out to intervene in history . . . failed . . . and paid the price. He knew he had a short time to live, as his epilepsy had become dangerously bad. By the end everyone had deserted him . . . except for faithful Mrs Rita Malan, this extraordinary woman whom he had never met.

My dear David, You have only one option now that no clemency may be expected: the rest of your days in the Criminal Lunatic Asylum. That's where they get rid of embarrassing cases (my son says). You will wear a pointed hat like a dunce and go up and down on your knees in your pyjamas, with a little board hung on your chest saying, 'I killed Verwoerd and he is forgotten now.' They will medicate you, because they are genuinely humane, but these will be the wrong medicines at the wrong times, and none of them will soothe the trouble in your soul. Your fits will become more frequent and take longer to subside, but at least orderlies will be around to hold you to the bed so that you do not damage yourself. Now that there is no mercy left, my dear, there is only one way.

I will always think of you, your bravery
With all my love.

SHERIF HETATA
Caravan

I walked across the bridge
Above my head dark clouds
Held their breath
Waiting
White herons
Fluttered their wings
Dipped their heads in the grey water
Looking for fish
Dawn crept over the sky
With stealth
Seemed pale, frightened, hesitant
Then the herons stopped their quest
Floating on the grey expanse
Motionless
And I stood there
A tiny dot
In the immense, wide open, yearning space
Living a lengthy pause
Living the taste of death

Suddenly they appeared
A caravan of camels moving fast
Sad faces
Looking out from glittering slits
Dark eyes
Like black fish
In a sea of melancholy
A hundred drooping flowers on wilted necks
Shifting sand dunes carried on loping legs
Whipped by nervous winds

Like a yellow forest
Drifting south

I saw him
Riding in front
At the prow of the ship
A pharaonic king
Disdainfully black
His body upright
Wrapped in white
Straight-backed
Moving up and down with the camel's lilt
I glimpsed his inscrutable eyes
Staring ahead
His hands around the fibre ropes
Guiding the caravan by touch
Lying loosely in his lap
Like birds in a nest

I saw its movement
A wave in space
Here one day
Gone the next
Crossing the bridge in the silver light
With him at its head
Splitting the universe
Oblivious to all else
One with it

He did not see me
Standing there in my training suit
Dressed in pink and red
Jogging shoes holding my feet
Bought from Oxford street, or somewhere else
He did not know I owned a Benz

Bought books
Arranged them on my shelf
Had money in the bank
Ate only toasted bread, for bread
Attended concerts twice a month
Believed in human rights and women's lib
Wrote about important things
Like justice

He left me standing there without a backward look
I watched him split the universe
Lift his eyes to the rising sun
Watched the yellow backs turn gold and red
As they fled
Wondered what it felt to ride on a camel's back
Into the sun

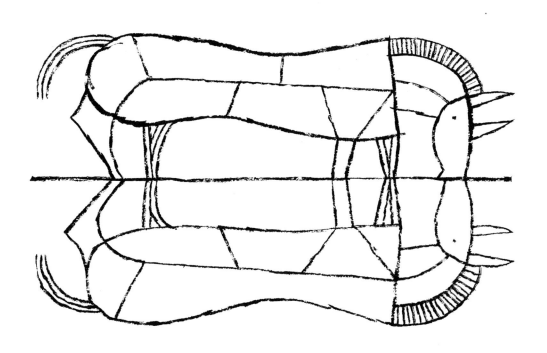

NADINE GORDIMER
Turning the Page . . .

In the beginning was the Word.

The Word was with God, signified God's word, the word that was Creation. But over the centuries of human culture the word has taken on other meanings, secular as well as religious. To have the word has come to be synonymous with ultimate authority, with prestige, with awesome, sometimes dangerous persuasion, to have Prime Time, a TV talk show, to have the gift of the gab as well as that of speaking in tongues.

As the 21st century approaches, the word flies through space, it is bounced from satellites, now nearer than it has ever been to the heaven from which it was believed to have come. But its most significant transformation occurred for us — the writers — long ago (*and* it was in Africa) when it was first scratched on a stone tablet or traced on papyrus, when it materialised from sound to spectacle, from being heard to being read as a series of signs, and then a script; and travelled through time from parchment to Gutenburg. For this is the genesis story of the writer. It is the story that *wrote* you or me into being.

It was, strangely, a double process, creating at the same time both the writer and the very purpose of the writer as a mutation in the agency of human culture. It was both ontogenesis as the origin and development *of* an individual being, and the adaptation, in the nature of that individual, specifically to the exploration of ontogenesis, the origin and development of *the* individual being. For we writers are evolved for that task. Like the prisoner incarcerated with the jaguar in Borges' story, 'The God's Script',[1] who was trying to read, in a ray of light which fell only once a day, the meaning of being from the markings on the animal's pelt, we spend our lives attempting to interpret through the word the readings we take in, the societies of which we are part. It is in this sense, this inextricable, ineffable participation, that writing is always and at once an exploration of self and of the world; of individual and collective being.

Writers in Africa in this century now coming to an end interpreted the greatest events on our continent since the abolition of slavery, from Things Falling Apart in the colonialist regimes, crossing the River Between oppression and liberation, passing Up in Arms through the Fog at the Season's End, Down Second Avenue, singing the Song of Lawino on the Mission to Kala, overcoming Nervous Conditions and discarding the Money Order as the price of bondage, enduring the House of Hunger, challenging the World of Strangers created by racism, recognising we were shirking responsibility as Fools for Blaming ourselves on History, confessing as An Albino Terrorist, telling us the Interpreters the Tough Tale of the struggle for Freedom.[2]

There is no prize offered for correctly identifying the writers of the books whose titles you should recognise strung together to tell the story in the account I have just given, nor will it be necessary to point out that these titles and writers are only a random few of those that have made manifest in our literature the embattled awakening of our continent.

We have known that our task was to bring to our people's consciousness and that of the world the true dimensions of racism and colonialism beyond those that can be reached by the media, the newspaper column and screen image, however valuable these may be. We writers have sought the fingerprint of flesh on history.

The odds against developing as a writer able to take on this huge responsibility have, for most of our writers, been great. But as Agostinho Neto said, and proved in his own life, 'If writing is one of the conditions of your being alive, you create that condition.'[3]

Out of adversity, out of oppression, in spite of everything.

Before we look forward into the 21st century we have the right to assess what we have come through. Being here; the particular time and place that has been 20th-century Africa. This has been an existential position with particular implications for literature; we have lived and worked through one of those fearful epochs Brecht has written of when 'to speak of trees is almost a crime'.[4] Our brothers and sisters have challenged us with the Polish poet Czeslaw Milosz's cry: 'What is poetry which does not serve nations or people?'[5] And we have taken up that challenge. Inevitably, the characteristic of African literature during the struggle against colonialism and, latterly, neo-colonialism and corruption in post-colonial societies, has been engagement – political engagement.

Now, unfortunately, many people see this concept of engagement as a limited category closed to the range of life reflected in literature; it is regarded as some sort of upmarket version of propaganda. Engagement is not understood for what it really has been, in the hands of honest and talented writers: the writer's exploration of the particular meaning of being has taken on in his or her time and place. For real 'engagement', for the writer, is not something set apart from the range of the creative imagination at the dictate of his brothers and sisters in the cause he or she shares with them; it comes from within the writer, his or her creative destiny as an agency of culture, living in history. 'Engagement' does not preclude the beauty of language, the complexity of human emotions; on the contrary, such literature must be able to use all these in order to be truly engaged with life, where the overwhelming factor in that life is political struggle.

While living and writing under these conditions in Africa some of us have seen our books lie for years unread in our own countries, banned, and we have gone on writing. Many writers have been imprisoned. Wole Soyinka, Ngugi wa Thiong'o, Jack Mapanje, Jeremy Cronin, Mongane Wally Serote, Breyten Breytenbach, Dennis Brutus, Jaki Seroke and a host of others. Many, such as Chinua Achebe and Nuruddin Farah, have endured the trauma of exile, from which some never recover as writers, and some do not survive at all. I think, among too many, of Can Themba and Dambudzo Marechera.

What has happened to writers in other parts of the world we cannot always dismiss as remote from being a threat to ourselves, either. In 1988, what the Greek novelist Nikos Kazantzakis called the 'fearsome rhythm of our time' quickened in an unprecedented frenzy, to which the writer was summoned to dance for his life.[6] There arose a threat against writers that takes its appalling authority from something more widespread than the power of any single political regime. The edicts of a world religion have sentenced a writer to death.

For three years now, wherever he is hidden, Salman Rushdie has existed under the pronouncement upon him of the *fatwa*. There is no asylum for him anywhere. Every time this writer sits down to write, he does not know if he will live through the day; he does not know whether the page will ever be filled. The murderous dictate invoking the power of international terrorism in the name of a great and respected religion is not something that happens to 'somebody else'. It is relevant to the themes that concern *us*, and will continue to do so, in African literature as part of worldwide post-colonial literature, for Rushdie's novel is an innovative exploration of one of the most intense experiences we share, the individual personality in transition between two cultures brought together in that post-colonial world. For the future freedom of the word, and for the human rights of all of us who write, the *fatwa* of death must be declared an offence against humanity and dealt with by those who alone have the power to do so – democratic governments everywhere, and the United Nations. The precedent of the *fatwa* casts a shadow over the free development of literature on our continent as it does everywhere, even as we believe ourselves to be moving into the enlightenment of the 21st century.

What do we in Africa hope to achieve, as writers, in the new century? Because we are writers, can we expect to realise literally, through our work, that symbol of change, the turning to a fresh page?

What are the conditions under which we may expect to write – ideological, material, social?

It seems to me that these are the two basic questions for the future of African literature, and what I hope to gain from this Conference is to hear them addressed from many points of view. I think it is generally agreed – it is surely one of the main reasons why we are gathered here – that consonance with the needs of the people is the imperative for the future in our view of African literature. This is surely the point of departure from the past; there, literature played the immeasurably valuable part of articulating the people's political struggle, but I do not believe it can be said to have enriched their lives with a literary culture. And I take it that our premise is that a literary culture is a people's right.

We shall all, as I have suggested, make the approach from our experience in the 20th century; we shall all be hazarding predictions, since we do not know in what circumstances our ambitions for a developing literature will need to be carried out. We have our ideas and convictions of how literary development should be consonant with these needs of our people; we cannot know with what manner of political and social orders we shall have to seek that consonance.

I think we have to be completely open-eyed about the relation between our two basic questions. We have to recognise that the first

273

— what we hope to achieve in terms of literary directions — is heavily dependent on the second: the conditions under which we shall be working as writers. A literary culture cannot be created by writers without readers. There are no readers without adequate education. It's as simple — and dire — as that. No matter how much we encourage writers who are able to fulfil, according to their talents, the various kinds and levels of writing that will take literature out of the forbidding context of unattainable intellectualism, we shall never succeed until there is a wide readership competent beyond school-primer and comic-book level. And where there are readers there must be libraries in which the new literature we hope to nurture, satisfying the need of identification with people's own daily lives, and the general literature that brings the great mind-opening works of the world to them, are available to them.

Will potential readers find prose, poetry and non-fiction in their mother tongues? If we are to create a 21st-century African literature, how is this to be done while publishing in African languages remains mainly confined to works prescribed for study, market-stall booklets, religious tracts? We have long accepted that Africa cannot, and so far as her people are concerned, has no desire to, create a 'pure' culture in linguistic terms; this is an anachronism when for purposes of material development the continent eagerly seeks means of technological development from all over the world. We all know that there is no such workable system as a purely indigenous economy once everyone wants computers and movie cassettes. Neither, in a future of increasing inter-continental contact, can there be a 'pure' indigenous culture. We see, a plain fact all over Africa, that the European languages that came with colonial conquest have been taken over into independence, *acquired* by Africans and made part and parcel of their own convenience and culture. The brilliant examples of this acquisition are there to be read in the work of some of the writers gathered here (Whites, of course, have never had the good sense to do the same with African languages . . .).

But we cannot speak of taking up the challenge of a new century for African literature unless we address the necessity to devise the means by which literature in African languages becomes the major component of the continent's literature. Without this one cannot speak of an African literature. It must be the basis of the cultural cross-currents that will both buffet and stimulate that literature.

What of publishing?

We write the books; to come alive they have to be available to be read. To be available, they have to be competently distributed, not only in terms of libraries, but also commercially. Many of us here have had experience of trying to meet the needs of the culturally marginalised by launching small, non-profit publishing ventures in African literature. We find ourselves stopped short by the fact that the distribution network, certainly in the Southern African countries (I don't imagine there is much difference in countries in the North) remains the old colonial one. Less than a handful of networks makes decisions, based on the lowest common denominator of literary value, on what books should be bought from publishers, and has the only means of distributing these widely to the public, since they own the chain bookstores which dominate the trade in the cities, and are the only existing book stores in most small towns. In South Africa, for example, in the 20th century, there have been and are virtually *no* bookstores in the vast areas where blacks have been confined under apartheid.

Another vital question: what will be the various African states' official attitude to culture, and to literature as an expression of that culture? We writers do not know, and have every reason to be uneasy. Certainly, in the 20th century of political struggle, state money has gone into guns, not books; literature, culture, has been relegated to the dispensable category. As for literacy, so long as people can read state decrees and the graffiti that defies them, that has been regarded as sufficient proficiency. As writers, do we envisage, for example, a dispensation from a Ministry of Culture to fund publishing in African languages, and to provide libraries in rural communities and in the shanty towns which no doubt will be with us, still, for a long time? Would we have to fear that, in return for subvention, writers might be restricted by censorship of one kind or another? How can we ensure that our implicit role – supplying a critique of society for the greater understanding and enrichment of life there – will be respected?

Considering all these factors that stand between the writer's act of transforming literature in response to a new era, it seems that we writers have, however reluctantly, to take on contingent responsibilities that should not be ours. We shall have to concern ourselves with the quality and direction of education – will our school turn out drones or thinkers? Shall we have access, through our writing, to young minds? How shall we press for a new policy and structure of publishing and distribution, so that writers may write in African languages and bring pleasure and fulfilment to thousands who are cut off from literature by lack of knowledge of European languages? How shall we make the function of writers, whose essential gesture, the hand held out to contribute to development, is in the books they offer, something recognised and given its value by the governing powers of the 21st century? We have to begin now to concern ourselves with the structures of society that contain culture, and within which it must assert its growth.

And there is yet one more problem to be faced by the naked power of the word, which is all we have, but which has proved itself unkillable by even the most horrible of conventional and unconventional weaponry. Looking back, many well-known factors inhibited the growth of a modern African culture, and African literature, in the century whose sands are running out through our fingers. One hardly need cite the contemptuous dismissal of all African culture by frontier and colonial domination; the cementing-over of African music, dance, myth, philosophy, religious beliefs and secular rituals: the very stuff on which literary imagination feeds. The creativity of African lay ignored beneath the trading feet of white people on their way to see the latest Hollywood gangster movie or to pick up from the corner store a comic with bubble text in American. And soon, soon, these were joined by black people in the same pursuit, having been convinced, since everything that was their own was said to be worthless, that this was the culture to acquire. The habit of chewing cultural pulp is by now so deeply established among our people, and so temptingly cheap to be bought from abroad by our media, including the dominant cultural medium of our time, television, that literature in Africa not only has to express the lives of the people, but also to assert the beauty and interest of this reality against the mega-culture that, in my revised terminology in a vastly changing world, is the opium of the people.

Surely the powers of the imagination of our writers can be exerted to attract our people away from the soporific sitcom, surely the great adventures that writers explore in life can offer a child something as exciting in image and word as the cumbersome battle between Japanese turtles? We do not want cultural freedom to be hijacked by the rush of international sub-literature into the space for growth hard-won by ourselves in the defeat of colonial cultures. That is perhaps the greatest hazard facing us as we turn the page of African literature and write the heading: 21st century.

Albert Camus wrote, 'One either serves the whole of man or one does not serve him at all. And if man needs bread and justice, he also needs pure beauty, which is the bread of his heart,' and so Camus called for 'Courage in one's life and talent in one's work'.[7] We shall need courage in our lives to take part in transforming social structures so that African literature may grow.

Gabriel Gárcia Marquez wrote, 'The best way a writer can serve a revolution is to write as well as he can.'[8] That goes for the peaceful revolution of culture, as well; without talent in our work, without ourselves writing as well as can, we shall not serve African literature as we should.

I believe that the statements of Camus and Marquez and Neto (remember his words: 'If writing is one of the conditions of your being alive, you create that condition') might be the credo for all of us who write in Africa. They do not resolve the conflicts that will continue to come, but they state plainly an honest possibility of doing so, they turn the face of the writers squarely to her and his existence, reason-to-be, as a writer, and the reason-to-be, as a responsible human being, acting like any other within a social and political context. Bread, justice, and the bread of the heart – which is the beauty of literature: these are all our business in Africa's 21st century.

This paper was delivered at the 'Symposium on the Main Issues in African Fiction and Poetry on the Threshold of the 21st Century', held in Harare, 10–13 February 1992. The Symposium was co-hosted by UNESCO, the Zimbabwe National Commission for UNESCO, the University of Zimbabwe and International PEN.

1 Jorge Luis Borges: 'The God's Script', *Labyrinths: Selected Stories and other Writings*, Donald H. Yates and James E. Kirkby (eds) (New York: New Directions Publishing, 1964).
2 Chinua Achebe: *Things Fall Apart* (London: Heinemann, 1958).
Ngugi wa Thiong'o: *The River Between* (London: Heinemann, 1965).
Chenjerai Hove: *Up In Arms* (Harare: Zimbabwe Publishing House, 1982).

Alex la Guma: *The Fog at the Season's End* (London: Heinemann, 1986).

Es'kia Mphahlele: *Down Second Avenue* (London: Faber and Faber, 1959).

Okot p'Bitek: *The Song of Lawino* (London: Heinemann, n.d.).

Mongo Beti: *Mission to Kala* (London: Heinemann, 1964).

Tsitsi Dangarembga: *Nervous Conditions* (Harare, Zimbabwe Publishing House, n.d.).

Sembene Ousmane: *The Money Order* (London: Heinemann, 1972).

Dambudzo Marechera: *House of Hunger* (Harare: Zimbabwe Publishing House, 1986).

Nadine Gordimer: *A World of Strangers* (London: Penguin Books, 1962).

Njabulo Ndebele: *Fools and Other Stories* (Johannesburg: Ravan Press, 1989).

Bloke Modisane: *Blame Me on History* (London: Thames and Hudson, 1963).

Breyten Breytenbach: *Confessions of an Albino Terrorist* (Emmerentia: Taurus, 1984).

Wole Soyinka: *The Interpreters* (London: Heinemann, 1970).

Mongane Wally Serote: *A Tough Tale* (London: Kliptown Books, 1987).

3 Agostinho Neto. From my notebooks; source not given.

4 From Bertolt Brecht: 'To Posterity', *Selected Poems*, trans. H. R. Hays (New York: Grove Press, n.d.).

5 Czeslaw Milosz: 'Dedication', *Selected Poems* (New York: Ecco Press, 1978).

6 Nikos Karantzakis: *Report to Greco* (London: Faber and Faber, 1965).

7 Albert Camus: *Carnets 1942–5*. n.p., n.d.

8 Garbriel Gárcìa Marquez: interview. From my notebooks, source not given.

Contributors' Notes

Ama Ata Aidoo has lectured in Ghana and consulted for universities in Africa, North America and Europe. She was Minister of Education in Ghana and currently lives in Harare, Zimbabwe. Her publications include novels: *Changes – A Love Story* and *Our Sister Killjoy or Reflections from a Black-Eyed Squint*; short story collections: *No Sweetness Here* and *The Eagle and the Chickens and Other Stories*; a drama: *The Dilemma of a Ghost*; collections of poetry: *Someone Talking to Sometime* and *Birds and Other Poems*.

Peter Amuka is head of the Literature Department at Moi University, Kenya. He is a former editor of *Busara*, Nairobi University's journal of creative and critical writing.

Ungulani Ba Ka Khosa is one of Mozambique's leading young writers.

Vusi Bhengu, **Goodman Kivan**, **Nester Luthuli**, **Gladman 'Myukuzane' Ngubo** and **November Marasta Shabalala** are well-known worker-performers from various communities in and around Durban, South Africa. They have been active in the emergence of a broadly based and mainly oral popular culture. Their work draws on a wide range of traditional and contemporary influences.

Dennis Brutus was born in Rhodesia (now Zimbabwe), educated in South Africa, and has spent many years in exile. He spent time on Robben Island, after being shot while attempting to escape detention. A central figure in the sporting boycott of South Africa and a prominent writer and critic, Brutus has published eleven books of poetry.

Shimmer Chinodya is the Zimbabwean author of four novels, *Dew in the Morning, Farai's Girls, Child of War* and *Harvest of Thorns*. He won the Commonwealth Literature Prize (Africa Region) and a Noma commendation in 1990.

Mia Couto currently lectures at the Edwardo Mondlane University in Maputo, Mozambique. Prior to this he was an award-winning journalist. His poems have appeared widely in Mozambican magazines and his published work includes a volume of poetry, *Raiz de orvalho*, and a collection of short stories, *Vozes Anoitecidas*, now available in translation as *Voices Made Night*.

Nadine Gordimer, Nobel Prize laureate, has published ten novels, over two hundred short stories and a collection of essays and addresses. The National Publicity Officer for the Congress of South African Writers, she has been deeply involved in, and committed to, the development of young writers' talents. Her novels include *A World of Strangers*, *A Guest of Honour*, *The Late Bourgeois World*, *Burger's Daughter*, *July's People*, *A Sport of Nature* and *My Son's Story*.

Stephen Gray has published several novels and poetry collections and edited numerous anthologies, re-issues of out-of-print works and critical studies of major writers. His novels include *Local Colour*, *Invisible People*, *Caltrop's Desire* and *Time of Our Darkness*. He has won a number of literary awards.

Liz Gunner, a South African, has lived in the Orange Free State, Natal Midlands and Northern Natal. She now teaches African Literature at London University and has recently – with Mafika Gwala – edited and translated a collection of Zulu poetry, *Musho! Zulu Popular Praises*.

Sherif Hetata is a writer and a medical doctor in Egypt. He has published six novels in Arabic, two of which were published in English by Zed Books. He has also translated works by his wife, writer Nawal el Saadawi. He spent fourteen years in prison for his political activities. He is now a full-time writer and a member of the Central Committee of the Progressive Arab Unionist Party.

Evelyn John Holtzhausen is a journalist, writing for the South African newspaper *The Sunday Times*, and has also worked in Swaziland, Norway and the United Kingdom. He has published poetry in *New Contrast*, and *Staffrider.*

Henry Indangasi has studied and taught literature at the University of Nairobi and the University of California, Santa Cruz. He is currently Chair of the Department of Literature at Nairobi University.

Jonathan Kariara is a well-known Kenyan poet. He has published critical writing and several collections of poetry. A founding editor of the East African Publishing House, Kariara now lectures on book publishing at Moi University.

Baleka Kgositsile, born in Durban, South Africa, started to compose poems and songs when she was ten years old and crossed the river from Fort Hare University, where her father was a librarian, to Lovedale, where she went to school. While in exile, her poetry was published in *Malibongwe, Rixaka, Somehow We Survive* and other publications. She is currently Secretary General of the African National Congress Women's League.

Keorapetse Kgositsile recently returned to South Africa, after thirty years in exile. He has studied and taught literature and creative writing in the USA and Africa. He has published six books of verse, *Spirits Unchained, For Melba, My Name is Afrika, The Present is a Dangerous Place to Live, Places and Bloodstains* and *When the Clouds Clear.* He has received a number of poetry awards and is currently vice-president of the Congress of South African Writers.

Mandla Langa lived, studied and worked in South Africa until 1976, when he was forced into exile. He currently works for the African National Congress in London. His published novels include *Tenderness of Blood* and *Rainbow on a Paper Sky.*

Arthur Luvai teaches literature at Maseno University College, Kenya. He has edited a volume of Kenyan poetry, *Boundless Voices*, and a children's anthology of stories and poems to mark the UN Year of the Child. His poems have appeared in several Kenyan anthologies and journals.

Zakes Mda is a well-known South African writer. He also paints and composes music. Previously based at the National University of Lesotho, he is currently a Research Fellow at Yale University.

Frank Meintjies works for the Community Based Development Project at the University of the Witwatersrand. He has published poetry, prose and critical writings in numerous journals and literary magazines. A volume of his poetry and prose is presently being published.

Madlinyoka ('snake-eater') Ntanzi is a prominent worker *imbongi* (bard) in Northern Natal. He stopped 'praising the chiefs' when he joined the Metal and Allied Workers' Union and has since been warmly received by audiences at rallies throughout Natal. The poem printed is different at every performance, as he adapts it to the rapid changes in South African politics.

Silas Obadiah is a Nigerian. His stories and poems have appeared in *Chelsea, Liwuram, The Greenfield Review, Obsidian II, The Literary Half-Yearly, The Seattle Review,* among others. He is currently participating in the Graduate Writing Programme of Brown University.

Tom Ochola lectures in literature at Maseno University College,

Kenya. His poetry has been published in a number of journals and collections. *Boundless Voices*, an anthology of Kenyan poetry, contains some of his recent work.

Tanure Ojaide is a Nigerian poet, translator and critic. He was winner of the Commonwealth Poetry Prize in 1987, the All-Africa Okigto Prize for Poetry in 1988 and the 1988 Overall Winner of the ESC Arts and Africa Poetry Award. His publications include *Children of Iroko, Labyrinths of the Delta, The Eagle's Vision, The Fate of Vultures* and *The Blood of Peace*. He currently teaches at the University of North Carolina.

Sterling Plumpp hails from Clinton, Mississippi. He is based at the University of Illinois, and his collections of poetry, prose and essays include *Portable Soul, Half Black, Half Blacker, Steps to Break the Circle, The Mojo Hands Call, I Must Go*, and *The Story Always Unfold* and an anthology of South African poetry, *Somehow We Survive*. He has won the Carl Sandburg Literary Award for Poetry.

Lesego Rampolokeng is one of the new generation of poets from Soweto. He has performed his own style of rap poetry at rallies and cultural events in South Africa and at the Zabalaza Festival in London. He has published a collection of poetry, *Horns for Hondo*, and his work has appeared in various literary magazines and journals.

Ari Sitas is a sociologist at Durban University, South Africa. Involved in trade union activities, he has been a central figure in the emergence of worker culture; directing plays, editing a volume of worker poetry, *Black Mamba Rising*, and initiating a range of organisations aimed at servicing cultural groups. A collection of his poetry, *Tropical Scars*, was published in 1989, and his novel, *William Zungu: A Christmas Story*, in 1991.

Cornelia E. Smith, born in a small village outside Johannesburg, was the second of nine children. Her father was a preacher in the Anglican Church. A qualified general nurse and midwife, she currently works in a private clinic.

Kelwyn Sole has worked in South Africa, Botswana and Namibia and studied in Johannesburg and London. He currently lectures in English at the University of Cape Town. His first collection of poetry, *The Blood of Our Silence*, won the Olive Schreiner Prize for Poetry and an honourable mention in the Noma Awards for Publishing in Africa. *Projections in the Past Tense*, his latest collection of poetry, is being published this year.

Wilma Stockenström is one of South Africa's foremost Afrikaans writers. She has published plays, poetry and novels, for which she has won a number of awards, including the Hertzog Prize. Her published works include *Laaste Middagmaal, Vir Die Bysiende Leser, Van Vergetelheid en Van Glans, Spieel Van Water, Uitdraai,* and *Die Kremetartekspedise.*

Ivan Vladislavić lives in Johannesburg and works as a freelance editor. His collection of short stories, *Missing Persons,* won the Olive Schreiner Prize in 1991. His first novel, *The Folly,* is due to be published by David Philip this year.

Frank Wilderson has published interviews, book reviews, poems, short stories and cultural criticism in journals, newspapers and anthologies. He has lived most of his life in the USA, but has also worked and studied in Trinidad, Morocco and Johannesburg. In 1988 he won the Maya Angelou Award for the Best Fiction Portraying the Black Experience in America.